United States Department of Agriculture
Forest Service
Research & Development
Southern Research Station
General Technical Report SRS-181

I0411703

Effects of Future Sulfate
and Nitrate Deposition Scenarios on
Linville Gorge and Shining Rock
Wildernesses

Katherine J. Elliott, James M. Vose, and William A Jackson

The Authors:

Katherine J. Elliott, Research Ecologist, Coweeta Hydrologic Laboratory, Center for Forest Watershed Science, SRS-4353, Southern Research Station, U.S. Department of Agriculture Forest Service, Otto, NC 28763; **James M. Vose**, Research Ecologist and Project Leader, Center for Integrated Forest Science and Synthesis, Southern Research Station, U.S. Department of Agriculture Forest Service, Raleigh, NC 27695; and **William A Jackson**, Air Quality Specialist, Air Resources Program, Region 8, U.S. Department of Agriculture Forest Service, Asheville, NC 28804.

Cover: LEFT: Lynville Gorge Wilderness; RIGHT: Shinning Rock Wilderness. From the collection of the U.S. Forest Service.

Product Disclaimer

The use of trade or firm names in this publication is for reader information and does not imply endorsement by the U.S. Department of Agriculture of any product or service.

October 2013

Southern Research Station
200 W. T. Weaver Blvd.
Asheville, NC 28804

www.srs fs.usda.gov

Effects of Future Sulfate and Nitrate Deposition Scenarios on Linville Gorge and Shining Rock Wildernesses

Katherine J. Elliott, James M. Vose, and William A Jackson

Effects of Future Sulfate and Nitrate Deposition Scenarios on Linville Gorge and Shining Rock Wildernesses

Katherine J. Elliott,[1] James M. Vose, and William A Jackson

ABSTRACT

We used the Nutrient Cycling Model (NuCM) to simulate the effects of various sulfur (S) and nitrogen (N) deposition scenarios on wilderness areas in Western North Carolina. Linville Gorge Wilderness (LGW) and Shining Rock Wilderness (SRW) were chosen because they are high elevation acidic cove forests and are located on geologic parent material known to be low in base cations and thus sensitive to acidic deposition. We used five sulfate (SO_4^{2-}) and nitrate (NO_3^-) deposition scenarios to compare with the current (base case) deposition: Scenario 1, SO_4^{2-} at 94 percent and NO_3^- at 95 percent of current deposition; Scenario 2, SO_4^{2-} at 58 percent and NO_3^- at 63 percent; Scenario 3, SO_4^{2-} at 42 percent and NO_3^- at 51 percent; Scenario 4, SO_4^{2-} at 35 percent and NO_3^- at 48 percent; and Scenario 5, SO_4^{2-} at 22 percent and NO_3^- at 48 percent. For both sites, soil exchangeable calcium (Ca^{2+}) increased while exchangeable aluminum (Al^{3+}) changed very little over the 90-year simulation period with greater reductions in SO_4^{2-} and NO_3^- deposition; and the increase in soil exchangeable Ca^{2+} improved soil Ca/Al molar ratios. Soil solution SO_4^{2-} was much lower at all soil depths with greater reductions in SO_4^{2-} and NO_3^- deposition. This reduction in SO_4^{2-} in solution resulted in greater soil solution acid neutralizing capacity (ANC). At LGW, soil solution ANC of shallow soil was improved with the deposition Scenarios 2-5 compared to current deposition. By 2040, solution ANC of deep soil had increased above $20\ \mu eq\ L^{-1}$ for Scenarios 3-5 at LGW suggesting that stream ANC will be improved as well with further reductions in acidic deposition. Soil and solution cation concentrations will be improved for both wildernesses based on Scenario 2; however, further reductions in acidic deposition (e.g., Scenario 5) will be needed to increase stream ANC to a level that could support trout and other fishes.

Keywords: Atmospheric deposition, calcium, forecasting, nitrogen, Nutrient Cycling Model, Southern Appalachians.

INTRODUCTION

The amendments to the Clean Air Act in 1977 and 1990 (especially Title IV) have significantly reduced emissions of sulfur dioxide (SO_2) and nitrogen oxides (NO_x) emitted into the atmosphere. As a consequence, the quality of the air that people breathe has improved as the National Ambient Air Quality Standards have been revised as new scientific information demonstrated the standards needed to be strengthened in order to protect public health. The Clean Air Act amendments of 1977 also designated certain wildernesses, national parks, and national wildlife refuges as Class I areas. These federally mandated Class I areas receive special protection from new sources of air pollution that could adversely impact the air quality related values, especially visibility. The 1990 amendments (section 169B) directed the U.S. Environmental Protection Agency (EPA) to issue regional haze rules. EPA fulfilled this direction in 1999 and implemented the Regional Haze Rule (64 FR 35713) to achieve the national goal of no human impact to visibility at the Class I areas by year 2064 set forth by the Clean Air Act amendments of 1977. In the Southeastern United States, the initial emphasis to make reasonable progress (by 2018) at achieving the national visibility goal will be to reduce SO_2 emissions, which are the main contributor to visibility impairment. Sulfur dioxide goes through a chemical transformation in the atmosphere to form fine particles of sulfates that reduce visibility and are eventually deposited on the tree canopy and ground as dry deposition. Acidic sulfur and nitrogen compounds are also deposited in the rainfall and snow, and at high elevations in the Eastern United States there can be very high concentrations in the cloud and fog water. It is unknown if the currently planned emissions reductions of air pollution, especially SO_2, will be sufficient to prevent or reverse the harmful effects from acidic deposition that have been reported at some wildernesses (Elliott and others 2008, Sullivan and others 2011a). In 2012, the EPA Administrator determined that the scientific uncertainty in the protection that would be achieved with a multi-pollutant secondary standard for oxides of nitrogen and sulfur was too great to establish a secondary standard to protect the public's welfare (such as aquatic biota) from the harmful effects of acidic deposition (http://www.regulations.gov/#!documentDetail;D=EPA-HQ-OAR-2007-1145-0205).

In this study, we used the Nutrient Cycling Model (NuCM) to simulate the effects of various sulfur (S) and nitrogen (N) deposition reduction scenarios to evaluate the potential

[1]Katherine J. Elliott is the corresponding author. To contact, call (828) 524-2128 or email at kelliott@fs.fed.us.

benefits that may be achieved for two federally mandated Class I areas in the Southern Appalachians of Western North Carolina. Linville Gorge Wilderness (LGW) and Shining Rock Wilderness (SRW) were chosen because they are high elevation acidic forests and are located on geologic parent material known to be low in base cations (Elliott and others 2008, Sullivan and others 2011a) and thus sensitive to acidic deposition. As part of the Integrated Forest Study, NuCM was developed to synthesize current understanding of nutrient cycling in forests and to predict how forests respond to changing S and N atmospheric deposition rates (Johnson and Lindberg 1992, Liu and others 1991a, 1991b). The NuCM model links soil-solution chemical components with traditional conceptual models of forest nutrient cycling on a stand level (Liu and others 1991a).

In an earlier study, Elliott and others (2008) used NuCM to simulate the effects of sulfur deposition on nutrient cycling at LGW and SRW. They simulated a 30-year period and used three sulfate (SO_4^{2-}) deposition scenarios—50 percent decrease, current condition, and 100 percent increase—but they did not include alterations of nitrate (NO_3^-) deposition. They suggested that even with large reductions in SO_4^{2-} and associated acid deposition that it may take decades before these systems recover from depletion of exchangeable cations (Elliott and others 2008). In our paper, we build on this previous work by including further reductions of SO_4^{2-} deposition, adding NO_3^- deposition reductions to the models, and running the simulations for a longer time period.

We used five SO_4^{2-} and NO_3^- deposition scenarios outlined in Sullivan and others (2011b). The five scenarios were based on results developed by the Visibility Improvement State and Tribal Association of the Southeast (VISTAS) to specify the base case emissions control scenario and associated levels of future acidic deposition at modeling site locations (Sullivan and others 2011b). VISTAS used the EPA Models-3 Community Multiscale Air Quality (CMAQ) modeling system (Byun and Ching 1999) and recently performed a technical analysis for the State, local, and tribal air quality agencies for ten Southeastern States (http://vistas-sesarm.org/documents/FinalDocs.asp). For each scenario, we simulated a 90-year period to forecast years 2010 to 2100. Our base case is the ambient deposition averaged from the last ten years of National Atmospheric Deposition Program (NADP) records (2002 to 2011). Future deposition scenarios used for our NuCM simulations and in previous studies modeling stream acid neutralizing capacity (ANC) (Sullivan and others 2004, 2011b) were:

Scenario 1—Reductions achieved under Title IV of the 1990 Clean Air Act Amendments—these were completed by 2006 (EPA/CMAQ from EPA reports)—constant after 2006;

Scenario 1, SO_4 at 94 percent, NO_3 at 95 percent of base case.

Scenario 2—2005 Clean Air Interstate Rule (CAIR) (http://www.epa.gov/cair/) in place for reductions from 2010–2020—EPA/CMAQ from National Acid Precipitation Assessment Program (NAPAP) 2005;

Scenario 2, SO_4 at 58 percent, NO_3 at 63 percent of base case.

Scenarios 3, 4, and 5—Reductions beyond CAIR based on additional rules, such as the 1999 Regional Haze Rule—EPA/CMAQ from NAPAP 2005;

Scenario 3, SO_4 at 42 percent, NO_3 at 51 percent of base case.
Scenario 4, SO_4 at 35 percent, NO_3 at 48 percent of base case.
Scenario 5, SO_4 at 22 percent, NO_3 at 48 percent of base case.

METHODS

Study sites

LGW and SRW are located in the southern portion of the Southern Appalachian Mountains; and they represent two of the four wilderness areas in Western North Carolina. Detailed descriptions of location, vegetation, soils, and geology for LGW and SRW are provided (table 1). LGW is one of the few remaining large areas of old-growth forest in the Eastern United States. LGW is an oak-pine old-growth forest (table 2). The soils are derived from lower quartzite, a material low in base cations and potentially sensitive to acid deposition. More detailed descriptions of the vegetation, geology, and soils in these wilderness areas can be found in Newell and Peet (1995). The catchment size used for our sampling within LGW was 24 ha; five 20 x 20-m plots were located along a 400-m transect from near stream to upslope from a first order stream that drained into the Linville River. Recently, the hemlock woolly adelgid (*Adelges tsugae* Annand) has caused widespread mortality of the Carolina (*Tsuga caroliniana* Engel.) and eastern hemlock (*Tsuga canadensis* (L.) Carrière) trees throughout the wilderness.

SRW is a former red spruce (*Picea rubens* Sarg.) forest; it was harvested and then severely burned by wildfires twice (1925 and 1942) (Vanderzanden and others 1999). Following the fires, there was extensive soil erosion which had additional negative impacts on base cation availability. SRW is currently a mixed hardwood forest (table 2). The soils are derived from lower quartzite, a material low in base cations and potentially sensitive to acid deposition. More detailed descriptions of the vegetation, geology, and soils in these wilderness areas can be found in Newell and Peet (1996).

Table 1—Site description of Linville Gorge Wilderness and Shining Rock Wilderness in Western North Carolina, USA

	Linville Gorge Wilderness	Shining Rock Wilderness
Location	Burke County in NC	Haywood County in NC
Mountain Range	Grandfather Mountains	Great Balsam Mountains
Size	4390 ha	7400 ha
Latitude	35.50 to 35.58	35.17 to 35.28
Longitude	81.56 to 81.52	82.59 to 82.47
Elevation	1090 – 1160 m	1450 – 1550 m
Geology	Lower quartzite	Mica gneiss
Soils	Typic Dystrochrepts; Soco-Ditney series complex	Typic Haplumbrepts; Wayah series
Climate		
Max temperatures	21 – 27 °C	27 – 30 °C
Min temperatures	14 – 17 °C	11 – 18 °C
Annual precipitation	1250 – 1625 mm	1025 – 1825 mm
Vegetation[a]	Acidic cove and slope (*Quercus montana, Pinus rigida, Pinus strobus*)	High elevation, mixed hardwood; subtype of northern hardwood forest (*Betula alleghaniensis, Acer rubrum*)
Mean DBH of overstory (range)	18.0 cm (5.0 – 71.1 cm)	12.8 cm (5.0 – 44.1 cm)
Aboveground mass	167 Mg ha^{-1}	119 Mg ha^{-1}
Forest floor mass	10,063 g m^{-2}	1,900 g m^{-2}
Root mass		1,000 g m^{-2}

[a]Linville Gorge, community type 3.1 (Newell and Peet 1995). Shining Rock, community type 5.2 (Newell and Peet 1996).

The catchment size used for our sampling within SRW was 62 ha; five 20 x 20-m plots were located along a 400-m transect at about 70-m intervals parallel to Greasy Cove Prong Creek (Elliott and others 2008).

The two wilderness areas differ in forest structure, species composition, and disturbance history. LGW is dominated by chestnut oak (*Quercus montana* Willd.), pitch pine (*Pinus rigida* Mill.), white pine (*Pinus strobus* L.), red maple (*Acer rubrum* L.), and sourwood (*Oxydendrum arboreum* (L.) De Candolle) with a less dense understory of evergreen rhododendron (*Rhododendron maximum* L.) and mountain laurel (*Kalmia latifolia* L.) than SRW (table 2). SRW is dominated by yellow birch (*Betula alleghaniensis* Britt.), red maple, mountain winterberry (*Ilex montana* Torrey & Gray), and pin cherry (*Prunus pensylvanica* L.) with a dense understory of evergreen and deciduous rhododendron species. For SRW, the last large-scale disturbance in 1942, a stand replacing fire, initiated the conversion from a *P. rubens* dominated forest to the present forest composition and structure (Vanderzanden and others 1999). Currently, the forest is comprised of northern hardwoods species that have

a windswept character, low stature and multiple branching pattern, and *P. rubens* is only a minor component of the forest community (table 2). The presence of the pine species at LGW contributed to the accumulation of forest floor mass (table 1). The recalcitrant evergreen litter at both LGW and SRW has contributed to the soil and soil solution acidity at these sites (tables 3 and 4).

Model Parameterization and Data Collection

Most of the model input data were derived from measurements taken at the five plots within LGW and SRW (Elliott and others 2008). Climate data were obtained from the National Climatic Data Center/National Oceanic and Atmospheric Administration (NCDC/ NOAA) climate station closest to each wilderness. For a complete description of data requirements for model parameterization see Munsen and others (1992). In brief, the NuCM model requires five input data files to parameterize the model for a simulation. These data input files include physiographic, chemistry, meteorologic, deposition, and soil temperature. The meteorologic, deposition, and soil

Table 2—Species composition, density (stems ha^{-1}), and basal area (BA; m^2 ha^{-1}) of the overstory (stems ≥ 5.1 cm dbh) and understory (stems < 5.1 cm dbh, > 0.5 m height) in order of descending basal area for Linville Gorge and Shining Rock Wildernesses in Western North Carolina, USA

Linville Gorge Wilderness					
Overstory	**Density**	**BA**	**Understory**	**Density**	**BA**
Quercus montana Willd.	90	6.15	*Rhododendron maximum* L.	450	0.42
Pinus rigida Miller	50	5.26	*Kalmia latifolia* L.	380	0.36
Pinus strobus L.	35	4.15	*Lyonia ligustrina* (L.) DC.	245	0.07
Acer rubrum L.	110	2.54	*Tsuga canadensis* (L.) Carr.	40	0.01
Oxydendrum arboretum (L.) DC.	185	2.51	*Oxydendrum arboretum* (L.) DC.	35	0.01
Nyssa sylvatica Marshall	135	2.30	*Symplocos tinctoria* (L.) L'Hér	20	0.01
Sassafras albidum (Nutt.) Nees.	190	2.10	*Pinus strobus* L.	5	0.01
Tsuga canadensis (L.) Carr.	25	2.01	*Nyssa sylvatica* Marshall	5	0.01
Magnolia fraseri Walter	10	0.36	*Amelanchier laevis* Wieg.	5	0.01
Quercus coccinea Muenchh.	10	0.30	*Sassafras albidum* (Nutt.) Nees.	15	<0.01
Hamamelis virginiana L.	55	0.22	*Acer rubrum* L.	5	<0.01
Amelanchier laevis Wieg.	15	0.19	*Rhododendron catawbiense* Michx.	5	<0.01
Castanea dentata (Marshall) Borkh.	15	0.09	*Hamamelis virginiana* L.	5	<0.01
Symplocos tinctoria (L.) L'Hér	10	0.04			
Quercus rubra L.	5	0.02			

Shining Rock Wilderness					
Overstory	**Density**	**BA**	**Understory**	**Density**	**BA**
Betula alleghaniensis Britton	280	4.22	*Rhododendron maximum* L.	715	1.42
Acer rubrum L.	45	2.64	*Vaccinium simulatum* L.	225	0.16
Ilex montana (T. & G.) A. Gray	700	2.40	*Ilex montana* (T. & G.) A. Gray	380	0.14
Prunus pensylvanica L. f.	245	2.37	*Rhododendron catawbiense* Michx.	90	0.08
Amelanchier laevis Wieg.	55	0.75	*Rhododendron calendulaceum* (Michx.) Torr.	220	0.07
Picea rubens Sarg.	5	0.53	*Clethra acuminata* Michx.	170	0.05
Acer saccharum Marshall	5	0.38	*Betula alleghaniensis* Britton	55	0.02
Betula lenta L.	5	0.12	*Kalmia latifolia* L.	10	0.04
Acer spicatum Lam.	5	0.02	*Viburnum nudum* (L.) var. *cassinoides* (L.) T. & G.	20	<0.01
			Rubus argutus Link.	20	<0.01
			Prunus pensylvanica L. f.	10	<0.01

Source: Linville Gorge and Shining Rock vegetation data from Elliott and others (2008).

Table 3—Soil chemistry for Linville Gorge and Shining Rock Wildernesses in Western North Carolina, USA

	Linville Gorge Wilderness (LGW)			Shining Rock Wilderness (SRW)		
	A-horizon (0-15 cm depth)	AB-horizon (15-35 cm depth)	B-horizon (35-65 cm depth)	A-horizon (0-20 cm depth)	AB-horizon (20-60 cm depth)	B-horizon (60-90 cm depth)
pH	3.45 (0.15)	3.91 (0.09)	3.95 (0.07)	3.41 (0.14)	3.85 (0.06)	4.11 (0.08)
NO_3^-	0.0003 (0.0003)	0.0003 (0.0003)	0.0002 (0.0001)	0.003 (0.002)	0.001 (0.001)	0.0003 (0.0002)
NH_4^+	0.005 (0.001)b	0.006 (0.001)b	0.004 (0.001)b	0.024 (0.008)a	0.018 (0.005)a	0.013 (0.002)a
PO_4^{2-}	0.011 (0.003)	0.004 (0.001)	0.003 (0.001)	0.010 (0.003)	0.003 (0.001)	0.003 (0.001)
K^+	0.116 (0.013)	0.082 (0.008)	0.063 (0.006)	0.162 (0.021)	0.090 (0.014)	0.059 (0.006)
Na^+	0.009 (0.001)	0.007 (0.001)	0.006 (0.001)	0.018 (0.003)	0.016 (0.001)	0.014 (0.001)
Ca^{2+}	0.039 (0.005)b	0.022 (0.004)b	0.018 (0.006)b	0.451 (0.070)a	0.161 (0.030)a	0.099 (0.020)a
Mg^{2+}	0.093 (0.007)b	0.043 (0.003)b	0.030 (0.004)	0.303 (0.068)a	0.109 (0.006)a	0.060 (0.004)
SO_4^{2-}	0.305 (0.104)b	0.556 (0.156)	0.404 (0.134)	0.187 (0.006)a	0.328 (0.012)	0.437 (0.008)
Al^{3+}	5.935 (0.658)	4.760 (0.473)	4.430 (0.571)	5.490 (1.316)	5.329 (0.408)	3.588 (0.757)
ECEC	6.84 (0.23)b	6.81 (0.40)b	5.46 (0.62)b	11.06 (1.64)a	10.29 (0.66)a	7.85 (0.56)a

Note: Standard errors are in parentheses. All values are in $cmol_c kg^{-1}$ except soil pH. Values within a soil horizon depth followed by different letters denote significant differences (α=0.05) between sites. Data from Elliott and others (2008). Exchangeable cations were extracted from 10 g of soil on a mechanical vacuum soil extractor using 50 ml of 1 $\underline{M}$ NH_4Cl. Solution concentrations of Ca^{2+}, Mg^{2+}, K^+, and Al^{3+} were determined with a Jobin Yvon Ultima Inductively Coupled Plasma Spectrometer (Horiba Inc., Edison, NJ) (Clescerl and others 1999). Following the initial 12-hour extraction excess NH_4Cl was removed from the soil interstitial spaces with 95% EtOH. NH_4^+-N on the soil exchange sites was then extracted with 2 $\underline{M}$ KCl as a measure of effective soil cation exchange capacity (ECEC).

Table 4—Mean soil solution and stream chemistry for Linville Gorge and Shining Rock Wildernesses in Western North Carolina, USA

	Linville Gorge Wilderness (LGW)				Shining Rock Wilderness (SRW)			
	A-horizon (0-15 cm depth)	AB-horizon (15-35 cm depth)	B-horizon (35-65 cm depth)	Stream	A-horizon (0-20 cm depth)	AB-horizon (20-60 cm depth)	B-horizon (60-90 cm depth)	Stream
pH	4.22 (0.12)	4.40 (0.12)	4.51 (0.11)a	4.74 (0.04)a	4.35 (0.15)	4.80 (0.11)	5.04 (0.09)b	6.08 (0.08)b
NO_3^--N	2.07 (0.89)	0.48 (0.12)a	0.62 (0.23)a	2.06 0.62)a	1.60 (0.75)	5.03 (1.75)b	5.68 (3.19)b	0.71 (0.12)b
NH_4^+-N	1.10 (0.49)	0.36 (0.05)	0.44 (0.15)	0.74 (0.18)a	0.93 (0.24)	1.67 (0.79)	0.57 (0.16)	0.35 (0.05)b
PO_4^{2-}	0.23 (0.08)	0.08 (0.01)	0.12 (0.01)	0.10 (0.01)	0.17 (0.04)	0.09 (0.02)	0.06 (0.01)	0.12 (0.02)
Cl^-	41.64 (5.97)	37.16 (4.12)	32.81 (2.82)	25.44 (2.34)a	55.38 (26.04)	43.16 (18.19)	21.56 (5.91)	7.99 (0.22)b
K^+	42.74 (8.05)a	17.16 (2.98)	9.68 (2.39)	7.35 (0.47)a	13.71 (2.84)b	6.08 (1.04)	4.17 (0.68)	5.29 (0.12)b
Na^+	23.82 (2.58)	23.60 (2.26)	17.69 (1.55)	18.36 (0.99)	20.19 (3.47)	16.47 (1.06)	17.15 (1.21)	25.62 (0.81)
Ca^{2+}	17.56 (4.60)	9.17 (2.56)	4.81 (1.98)	13.80 (3.01)	22.74 (5.26)	22.32 (4.04)	17.66 (2.99)	15.28 (2.03)
Mg^{2+}	30.76 (3.84)	22.45 (4.13)	15.81 (3.45)	15.14 (1.16)	29.89 (6.73)	20.46 (1.83)	19.50 (2.56)	12.15 (0.79)
SO_4^{2-}	99.98 (7.63)	113.1 (11.23)a	91.80 (12.26)	51.95 (0.44)a	64.18 (22.50)	42.34 (5.06)b	38.79 (4.16)	19.82 (0.62)b
Al	118.0 (18.49)	89.06 (20.02)	69.09 (14.80)a	17.61 (1.20)	140.7 (50.58)	37.96 (11.71)	24.48 (6.23)b	31.01 (17.57)
DOC	26.52 (6.97)	11.21 (4.23)	6.64 (2.45)	1.37 (0.20)	15.54 (4.75)	2.47 (0.54)	1.61 (0.32)	1.47 (0.17)

Note: Standard errors are in parentheses. All values are in $\mu eq\ L^{-1}$ except for soil pH and DOC (mg L^{-1}). Values within a soil horizon depth or stream followed by different letters denote significant differences (α=0.05) between sites. Data from Elliott and others (2008).

temperature data were created outside the model and input as ASCII files, whereas the physiographic and chemistry files were created through input menus within the model. The meteorologic data file contains daily values for precipitation, minimum and maximum temperature, cloud cover, dewpoint, atmospheric pressure, and wind speed. For LGW, precipitation data were obtained from Banner Elk, NC (NCDC/NOAA climate station #310506) located at 36.09 N latitude, 81.52 W longitude, and 1142 m elevation. Maximum and minimum temperature, wind speed, dew point, and cloud cover were obtained from Jefferson, NC (NCDC/NOAA, climate station #314496) located at 36.25 N latitude, 81.26 W longitude, and 845 m elevation. Banner Elk is located about 14 km and Jefferson is about 70 km north of LGW. Banner Elk only collected precipitation, but its precipitation would be more similar to that received at LGW. Jefferson was the closest climate station with a full climate record. For SRW, climate data were obtained from Pisgah, NC (NCDC/NOAA climate station #316805), located at 35.16 N latitude, 83.42 W longitude, and 645 m elevation, and approximately 16 km southeast of SRW. We used average annual daily means for the 10-year climate record from 2002 to 2011 for both LGW and SRW. We used atmospheric deposition data, bulk deposition wetfall and dryfall, for a 10-year period (2002 to 2011), supplied from National Atmospheric Deposition Program (NADP 1998) site NC45 located at Mt. Mitchell, NC. Mt. Mitchell is the closest NADP site to LGW and SRW and it is also a high elevation site (1900 m). Wet deposition (wetfall) and dry deposition (dryfall) were calculated from a ratio of wetfall/dryfall based on the long-term record at Coweeta Hydrologic Laboratory. Soil temperature data were calculated from air temperature data using a model developed for the Coweeta Basin (Vose and Swank 1991); monthly average values were calculated for each of the soil depths used in the simulations. Model input data included stand physical characteristics (tables 1 and 2), soil physical characteristics, soil and soil solution chemistry (tables 3 and 4), and stream chemistry (table 4). Aboveground live biomass and root biomass estimated values were obtained from previous research in LGW and SRW (Elliott and others 2008). Once compiled, these data were input using the format outlined in the NuCM User's Manual (Munsen and others 1992).

RESULTS AND DISCUSSION

In the Southern Appalachians, ecosystem sensitivity to the potential effects of acidic deposition on nutrient status of forest soils and surface water quality has been well studied (Baker and others 1990, Elliott and others 2008, Johnson

and others 1999, NAPAP 2005, Sullivan and others 2004). Hydrogen ions associated with S and N deposition replace nutrient base cations (Ca^{2+}, Mg^{2+}, and K^+) on soil cation exchange sites. When base cations become mobilized they are leached into drainage waters, leaving soils with depleted stores of nutrient base cations. Soils in this region with decreased exchangeable base cation and increased available Al due to acidic deposition have been shown to alter the health and productivity of forest trees (Halman and others 2011, Long and others 2011, Schaberg and others 2006).

LGW and SRW contain ecosystems where acidic deposition has depleted soil base cation supply. This reduced soil buffering capacity and continued acidic deposition have resulted in unsuitable stream water pH and ANC conditions for the survival of many fish and macroinvertebrate species. Initial soil NH_4^+, Ca^{2+}, Mg^{2+}, and effective cation exchange capacity (ECEC) were lower at LGW than at SRW, whereas soil SO_4^{2-} was greater at LGW (table 3). Soil solution and stream chemistry were also different between the two wilderness areas (table 4). In general, LGW had much lower soil solution base cation and greater acid anion concentrations than SRW (table 4). Al and SO_4^{2-}, and NO_3^- solution concentrations were significantly greater at LGW than at SRW.

Stream SO_4^{2-} concentration was also greater at LGW than at SRW (table 4). At LGW, stream SO_4^{2-} concentration was higher than the mean values observed at Noland Divide in the Great Smoky Mountains National Park (Robinson and others 2003). Stream NO_3^- concentrations at both LGW and SRW were an order of magnitude lower than that reported for Noland Divide (Robinson and others 2003). The pH of stream water at LGW was significantly lower than at SRW and much less than pH values recorded at reference watershed streams at the Coweeta Long Term Ecological Research (LTER) site (Swank and Waide 1988). Low pH and high Al concentrations have been shown to diminish species diversity and the abundance of invertebrates and fish in acid-impacted surface waters in the Northeast (Driscoll and others 2003). The extremely low pH and high Al concentrations of the first order streams at LGW may be harmful to aquatic biota in this wilderness. For example, in the Adirondack region of New York, lakes with pH between 4.0 and 5.0 supported one or two species of fish on average, whereas lakes with pH ranging from 5.0 to 8.0 supported between three and six species of fish (Driscoll and others 2001). Low stream ANC has also been associated with negative impacts to aquatic biota and fisheries, especially native brook trout, *Salvelinus fontinalis* (Cosby and others 2006). The ANC value at SRW (28.8 μeq L^{-1}) suggests that this site is extremely sensitive to further acidification and may adversely affect brook trout. The ANC value (-24.8 μeq L^{-1}) at LGW indicates that this stream is no longer able to support brook trout or any fish species because acid inputs can no longer be neutralized (Bulger and others 1999).

We found very little difference in soil, soil solution, or stream water chemistry between the current (base) deposition and Scenario 1 deposition over the 90-year simulation (figs. 1-24) because SO_4^{2-} and NO_3^- depositions were reduced only slightly (-6 percent) for the Scenario 1 forecast (Sullivan and others 2011b). For this reason, we discuss only Scenarios 2-5 in comparison to the base deposition and among each other.

For the shallow soil depth (A-horizon), soil base saturation (BS) increased up to year 2030 then gradually declined at both sites (figs. 1 and 2). BS was more than 2 percent higher for Scenario 5 (greatest SO_4^{2-} and NO_3^- deposition reductions) than the base deposition scenario at LGW (fig. 1), and 8 percent higher at SRW (fig. 2). For the deeper soils (AB- and B-horizons), BS lagged behind the response in the shallow soil, and not until 2040 were there differences among the deposition reduction scenarios at LGW (fig. 1). BS in the AB-horizon increased at SRW over time for all scenarios (fig. 2); whereas, BS declined at LGW at the deeper soil depths (fig. 1).

For both sites, soil exchangeable Ca^{2+} increased (figs. 3 and 4) while exchangeable Al^{3+} changed very little (figs. 5 and 6) with greater reductions in SO_4^{2-} and NO_3^- deposition. Soil adsorbed SO_4^{2-} incrementally decreased as SO_4^{2-} and NO_3^- deposition was reduced (Scenarios 2-4) and was lowest for Scenario 5 at LGW (fig. 7) and SRW (fig. 8). The increase in exchangeable Ca^{2+} improved soil Ca/Al molar ratios (figs. 9 and 10). Simulated Ca/Al ratios in A-horizon soils for LGW and SRW were similar to ratios found at Noland Divide, a high-elevation, spruce-fir forest in the Great Smoky Mountains National Park (Johnson and others 1999). Even after the 90-year simulation for all deposition scenarios, soil exchangeable Ca^{2+} concentrations at LGW and SRW were still quite low ($\leq$1.0 cmol$_c$ Ca kg^{-1}) and were comparable to those reported for acidic soils in hardwood forests (0.7-0.8 cmol$_c$ Ca kg^{-1}) in West Virginia (Farr and others 2009), pine forests (0.05-0.23 cmol$_c$ Ca kg^{-1}) in South Carolina (Markewitz and others 1998), and hardwood forests (0.8 cmol$_c$ Ca kg^{-1}) in Tennessee (Johnson and others 2008).

Soil solution Ca^{2+} concentrations were higher for the shallow soils with greater reductions in SO_4^{2-} and NO_3^- deposition at both sites (figs. 11 and 12). Soil solution Al was much lower

at both sites with the greatest reduction in SO_4^{2-} and NO_3^- deposition, Scenario 5 (figs. 13 and 14). However, solution Al concentrations at LGW remain 4-5 times higher than at SRW regardless of the deposition scenarios.

For both sites, soil solution SO_4^{2-} was much lower at all soil depths with greater reductions in SO_4^{2-} and NO_3^- deposition (figs. 15 and 16). This reduction in solution SO_4^{2-} resulted in greater soil solution ANC (figs. 17 and 18). At LGW, soil solution ANC of shallow soil was improved with the deposition Scenarios 2-5 compared to base scenario deposition (fig. 17). By 2040, solution ANC of deep soil had increased above 20 μeq L^{-1} for Scenarios 3-5 at LGW suggesting that stream ANC will be improved as well with further reductions in acidic deposition.

For LGW, Ca^{2+} leaching declined rapidly until year 2040; thereafter Ca^{2+} leaching began to rise until year 2060 where it plateaued (fig. 19). For SRW, Ca^{2+} leaching increased over time with the base deposition and declined gradually for Scenarios 2-5 with the greatest reduction with Scenario 5 (fig. 20). Aluminum leaching was reduced substantially with the greatest reductions in acidic deposition at both wildernesses (figs. 21 and 22). Within 10 years of simulations, Al leaching was 0.08 kmols ha^{-1} yr^{-1} lower at LGW (fig. 21) and 0.01 kmols ha^{-1} yr^{-1} lower at SRW (fig. 22) for Scenario 5 compared to the base deposition. By the end of the 90-year simulation, Al leaching was reduced by 0.14 kmols ha^{-1} yr^{-1} at LGW and 0.04 kmols ha^{-1} yr^{-1} at SRW with Scenario 5.

Soil and solution cation concentrations are expected to improve within both wilderness areas based on CAIR emissions reductions (Scenario 2); however, further reductions in acidic deposition (e.g., Scenario 5) will be needed to increase stream ANC to a level that could support trout and other fishes (Bulger and others 1999). By 2050, SO_4^{2-} leaching was reduced by 37 percent at LGW (fig. 23) and by 40 percent at SRW (fig. 24) with CAIR provisions. SO_4^{2-} leaching would be reduced even further if Scenario 5 provisions were adopted, by 66 percent and 68 percent at LGW and SRW, respectively. Substantial SO_2 emission reductions are also known to be occurring in Georgia, South Carolina, and Tennessee. Therefore, there is a strong possibility that sulfur deposition will be reduced to a level above Scenario 4 and more likely close to Scenario 5. Nitrogen oxides emissions are also projected to decrease, but the percent reduction between 2002 and 2018 is unlikely to be as large as SO_2.

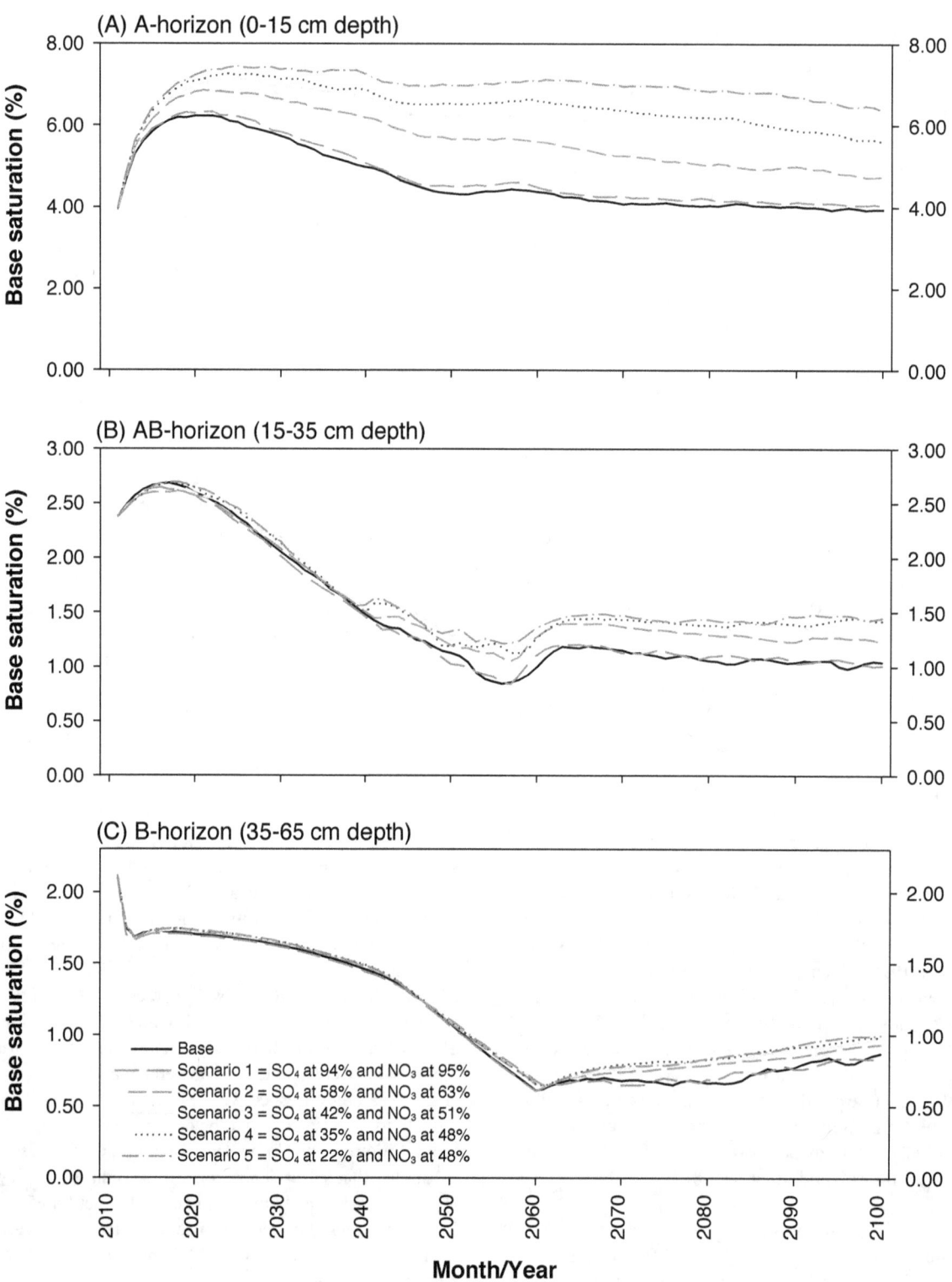

Figure 1—Simulated soil base saturation for five deposition scenarios compared to the current deposition (base) for Linville Gorge Wilderness. The five scenarios were based on percentages of the current condition.

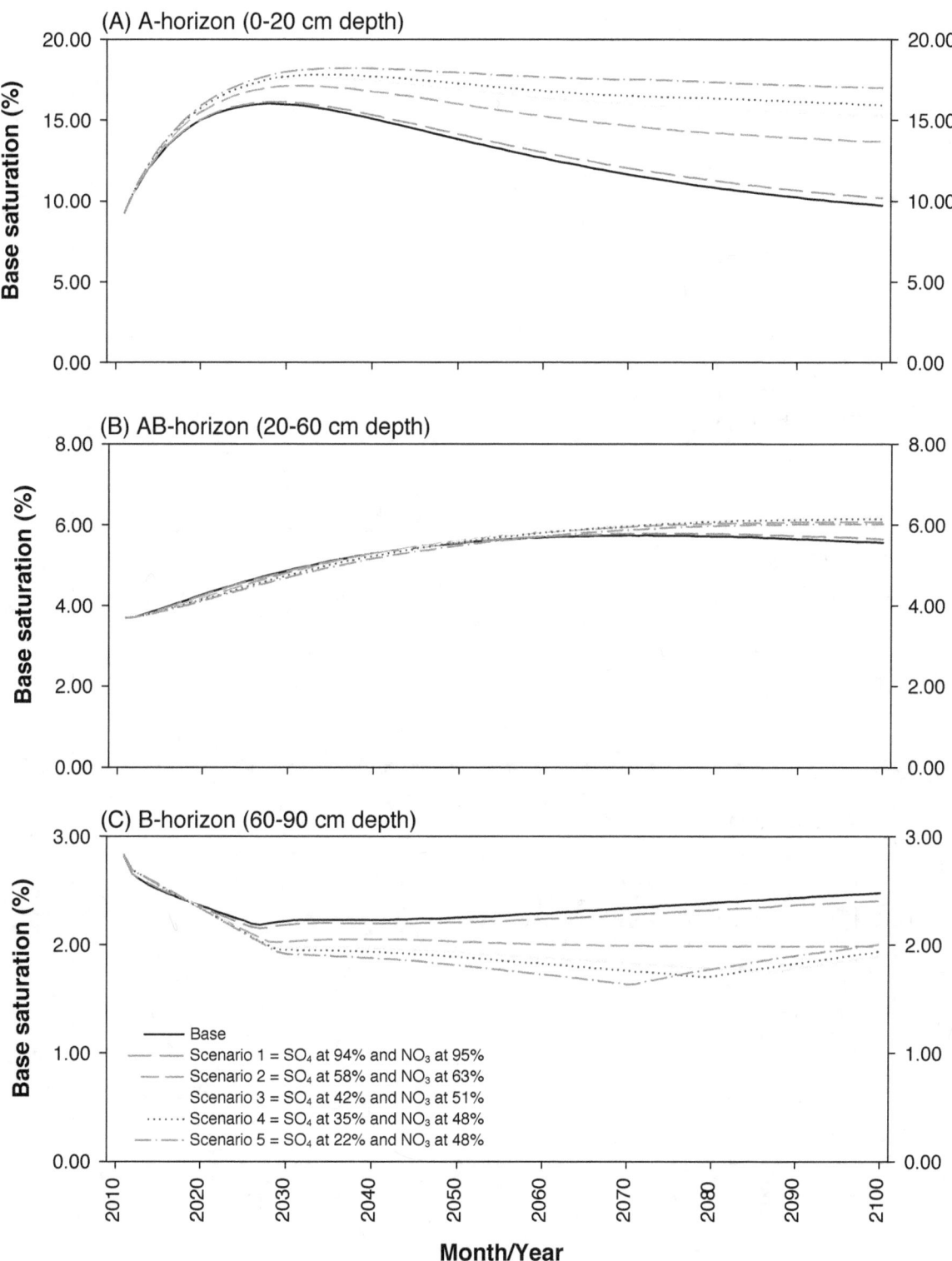

Figure 2—Simulated soil base saturation for the five deposition scenarios compared to the current deposition (base) for Shining Rock Wilderness. The five scenarios were based on percentages of the current condition.

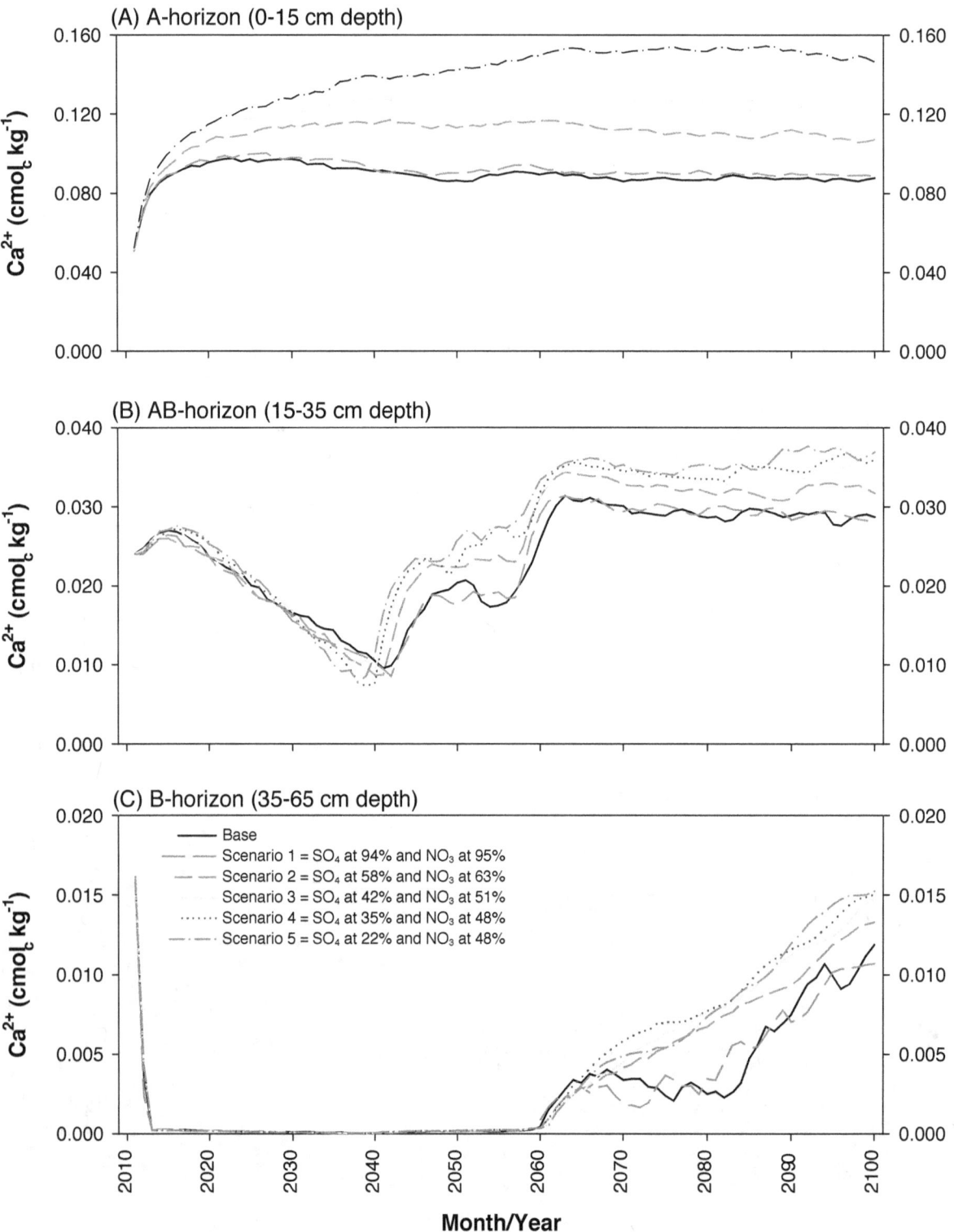

Figure 3—Simulated soil exchangeable calcium (Ca²⁺) for the five deposition scenarios compared to the current deposition (base) for Linville Gorge Wilderness. The five scenarios were based on percentages of the current condition.

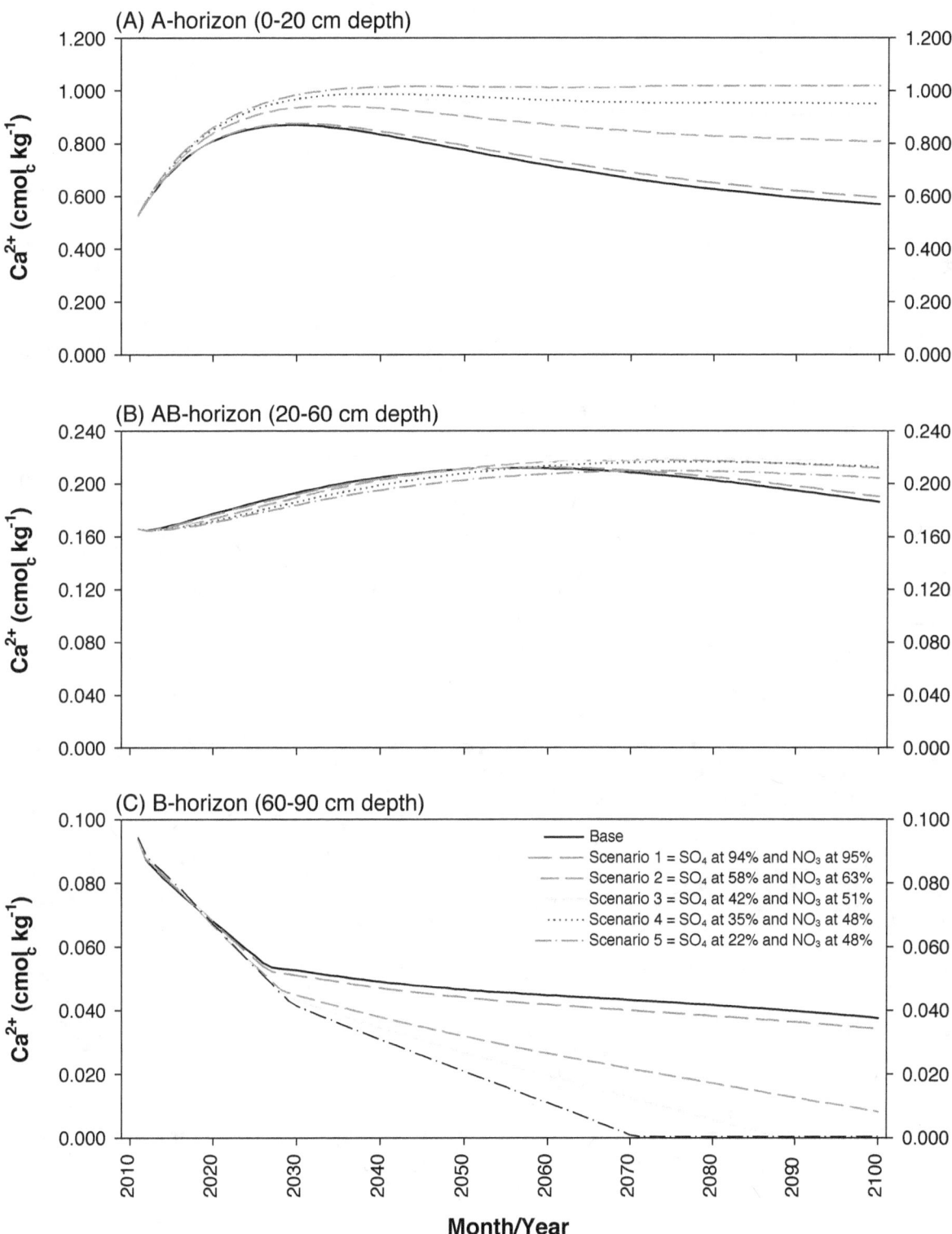

Figure 4—Simulated soil exchangeable calcium (Ca^{2+}) for the five deposition scenarios compared to the current deposition (base) for Shining Rock Wilderness. The five scenarios were based on percentages of the current condition.

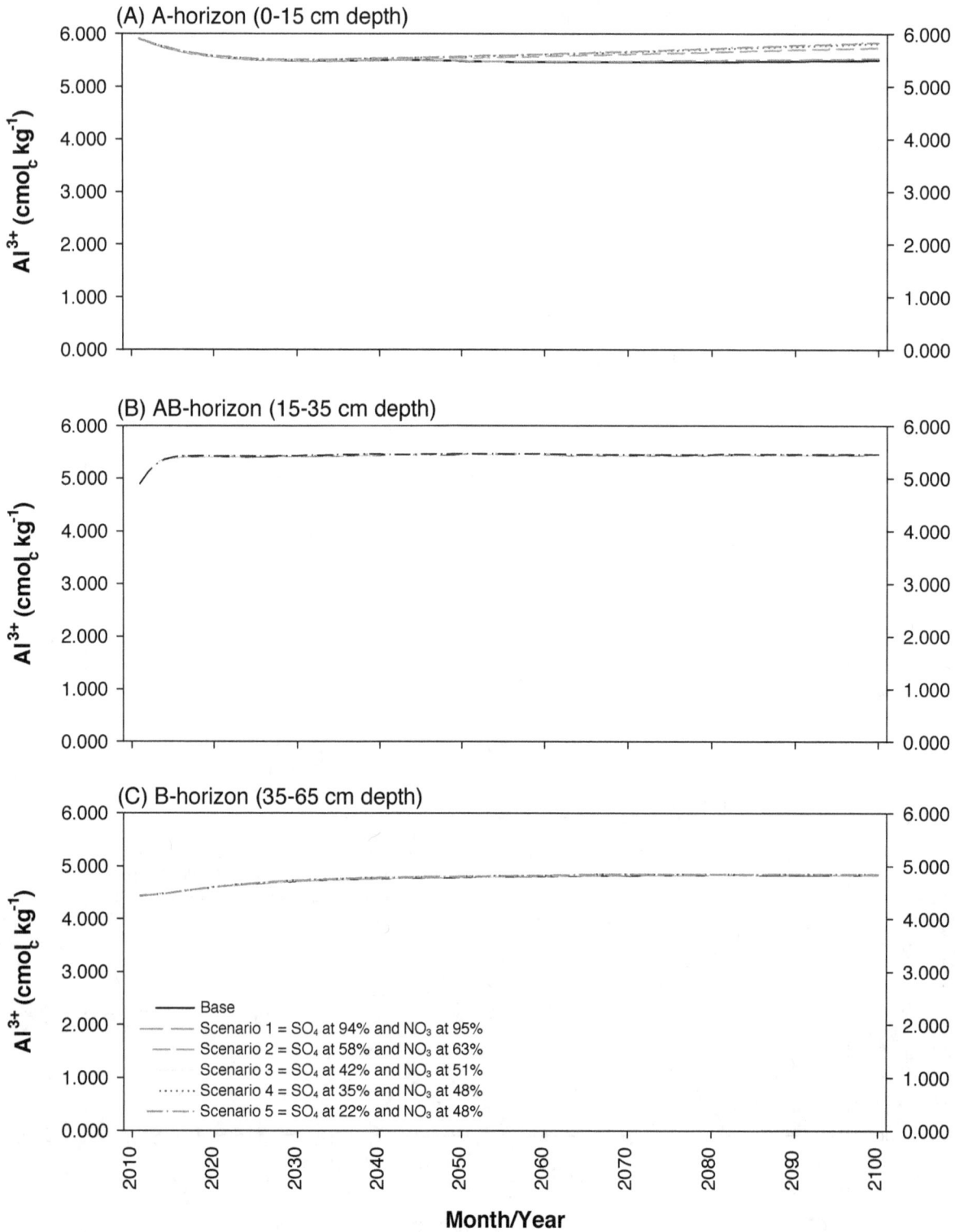

Figure 5—Simulated soil exchangeable aluminum (Al^{3+}) for the five deposition scenarios compared to the current deposition (base) for Linville Gorge Wilderness. The five scenarios were based on percentages of the current condition.

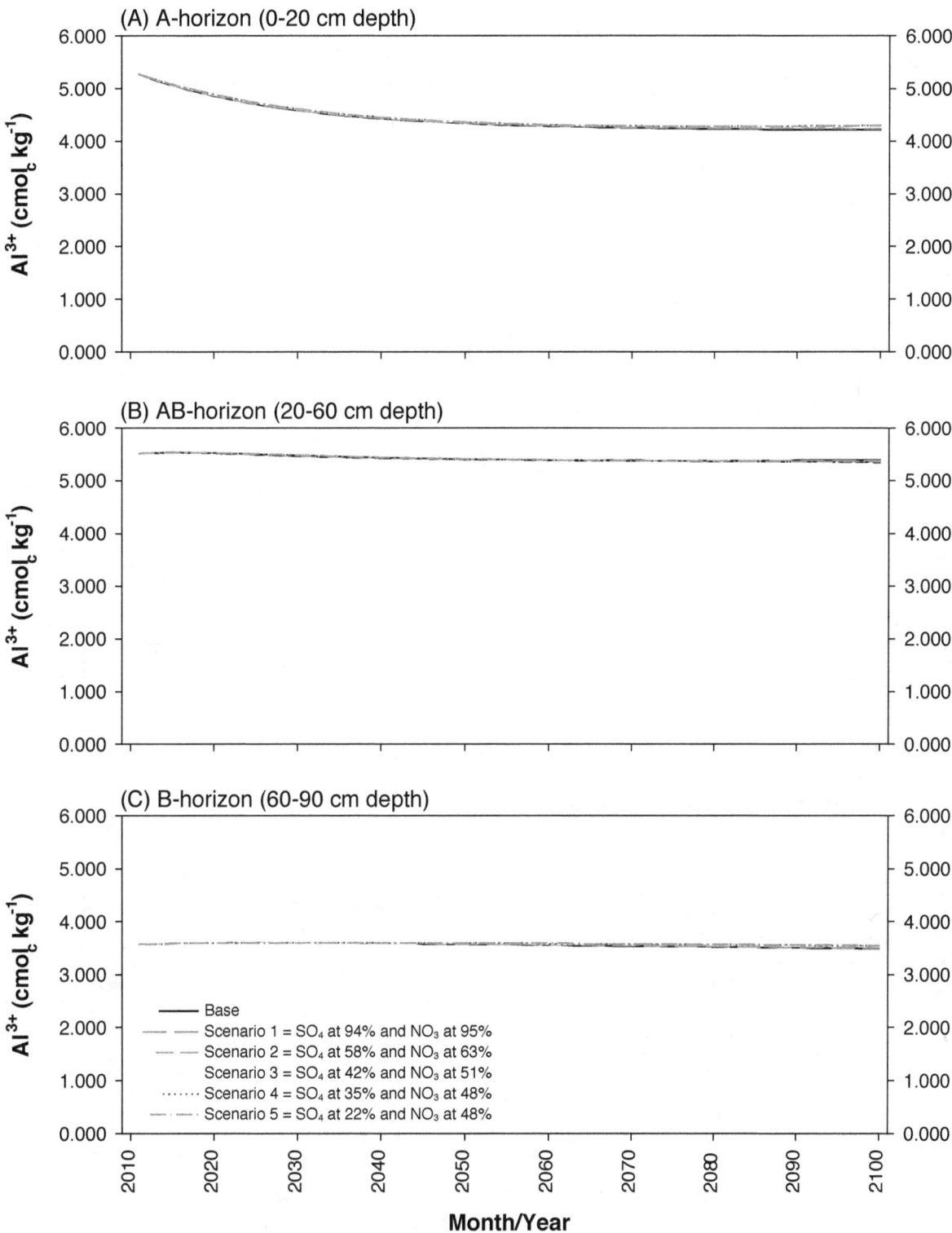

Figure 6—Simulated soil exchangeable aluminum (Al³⁺) for the five deposition scenarios compared to the current deposition (base) for Shining Rock Wilderness. The five scenarios were based on percentages of the current condition.

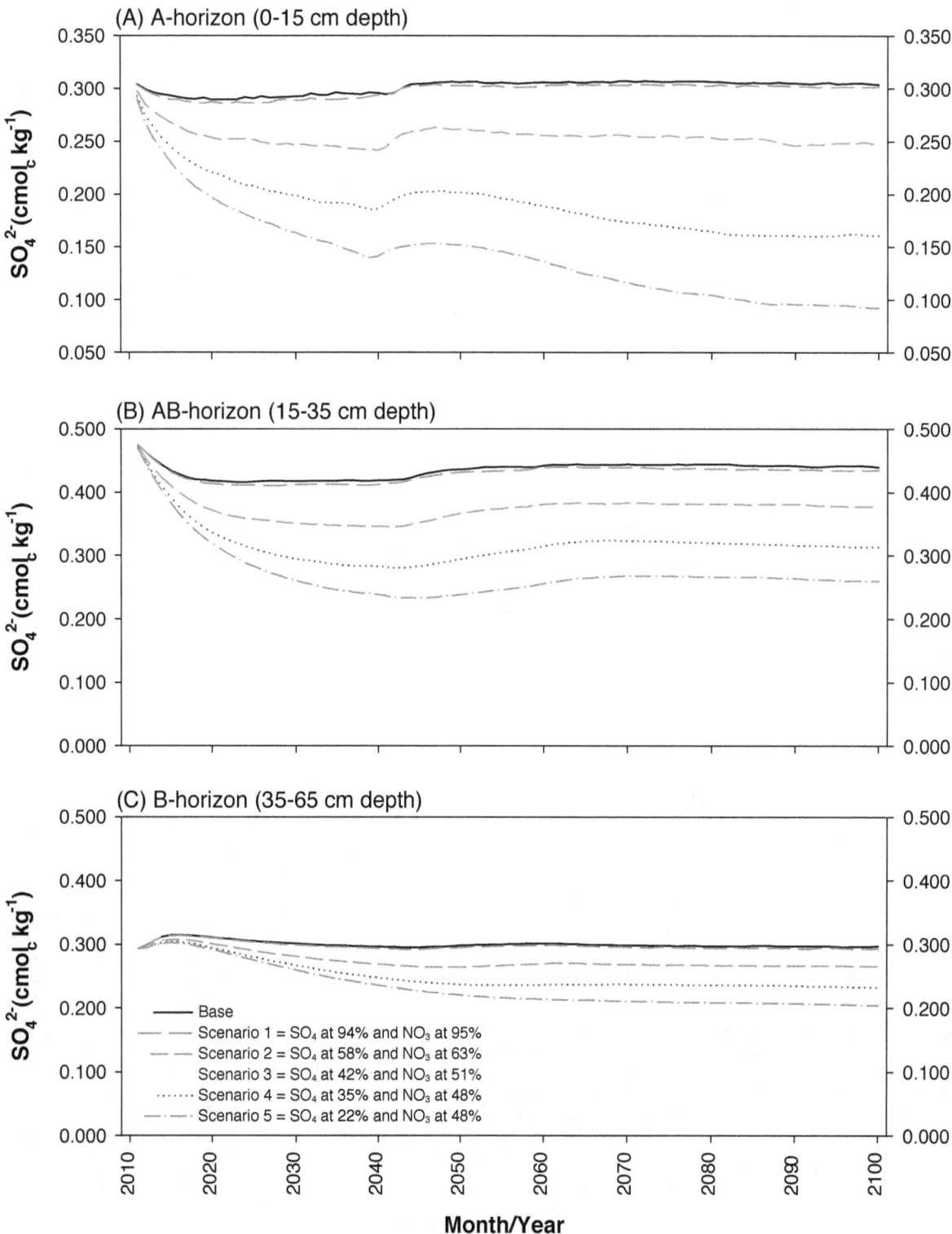

Figure 7—Simulated soil adsorbed sulfate (SO$_4$$^{2-}$) for the five deposition scenarios compared to the current deposition (base) for Linville Gorge Wilderness. The five scenarios were based on percentages of the current condition.

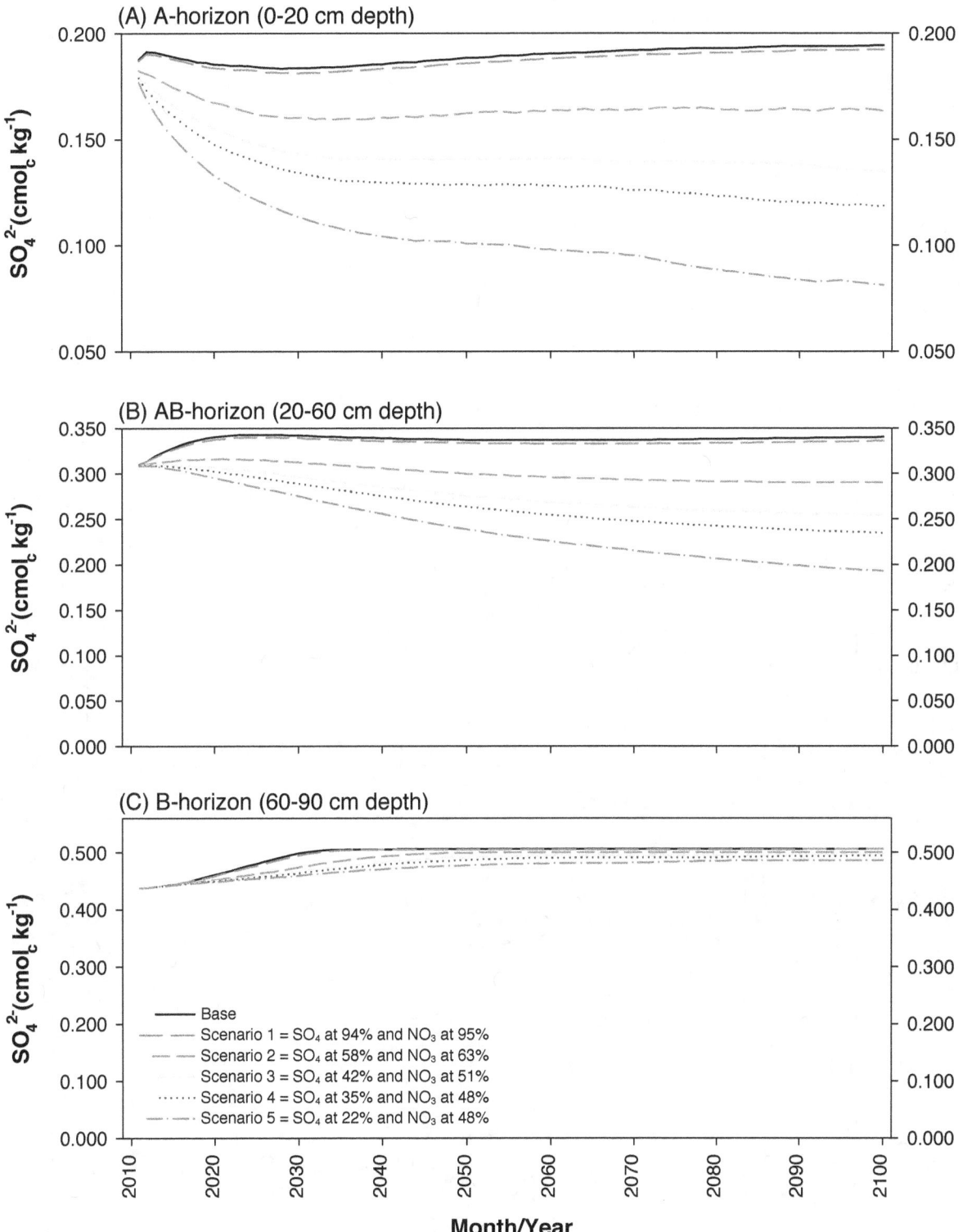

Figure 8—Simulated soil adsorbed sulfate (SO_4^{2-}) for the five deposition scenarios compared to the current deposition (base) for Shining Rock Wilderness. The five scenarios were based on percentages of the current condition.

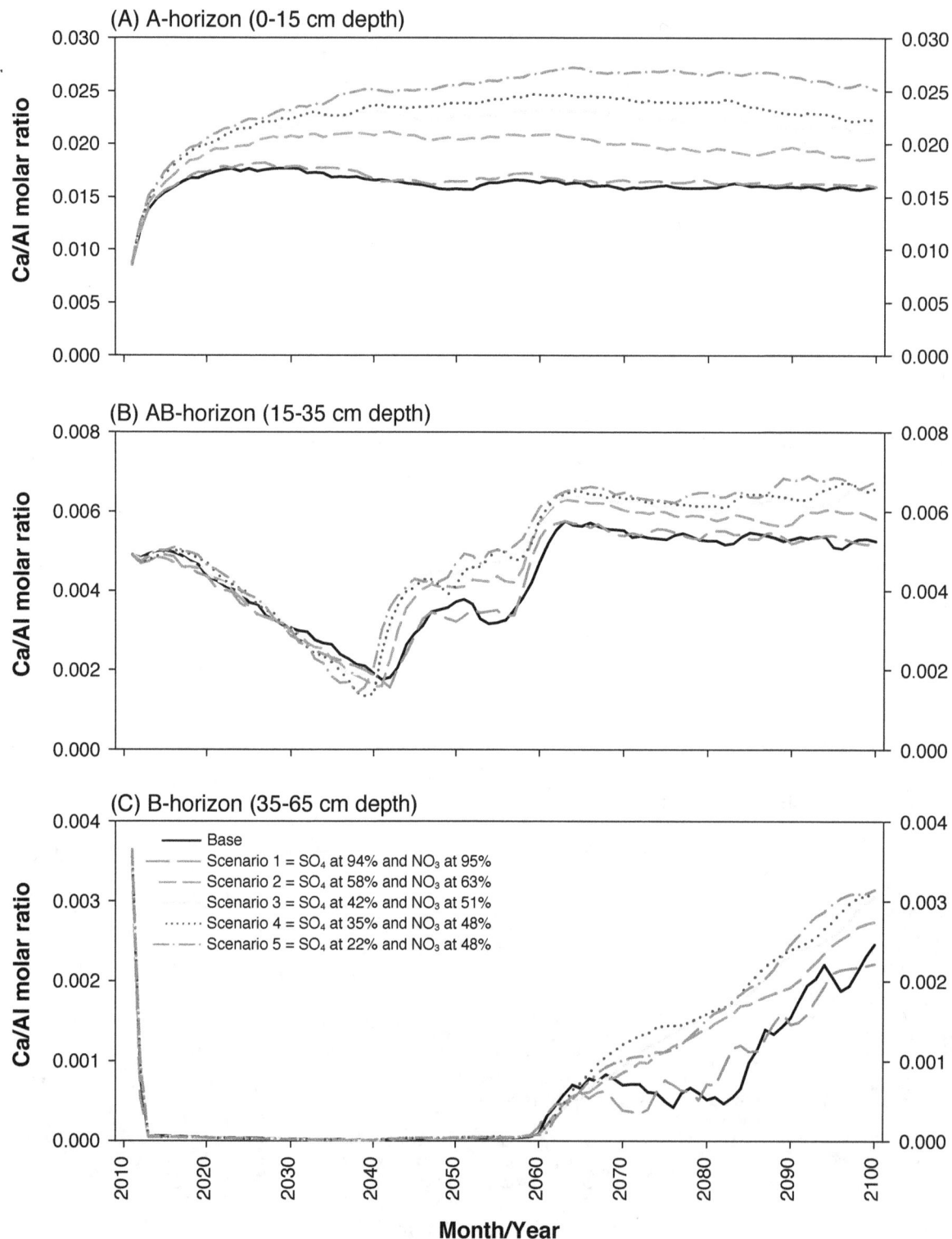

Figure 9—Simulated soil Ca/Al molar ratio for the five deposition scenarios compared to the current deposition (base) for Linville Gorge Wilderness. The five scenarios were based on percentages of the current condition.

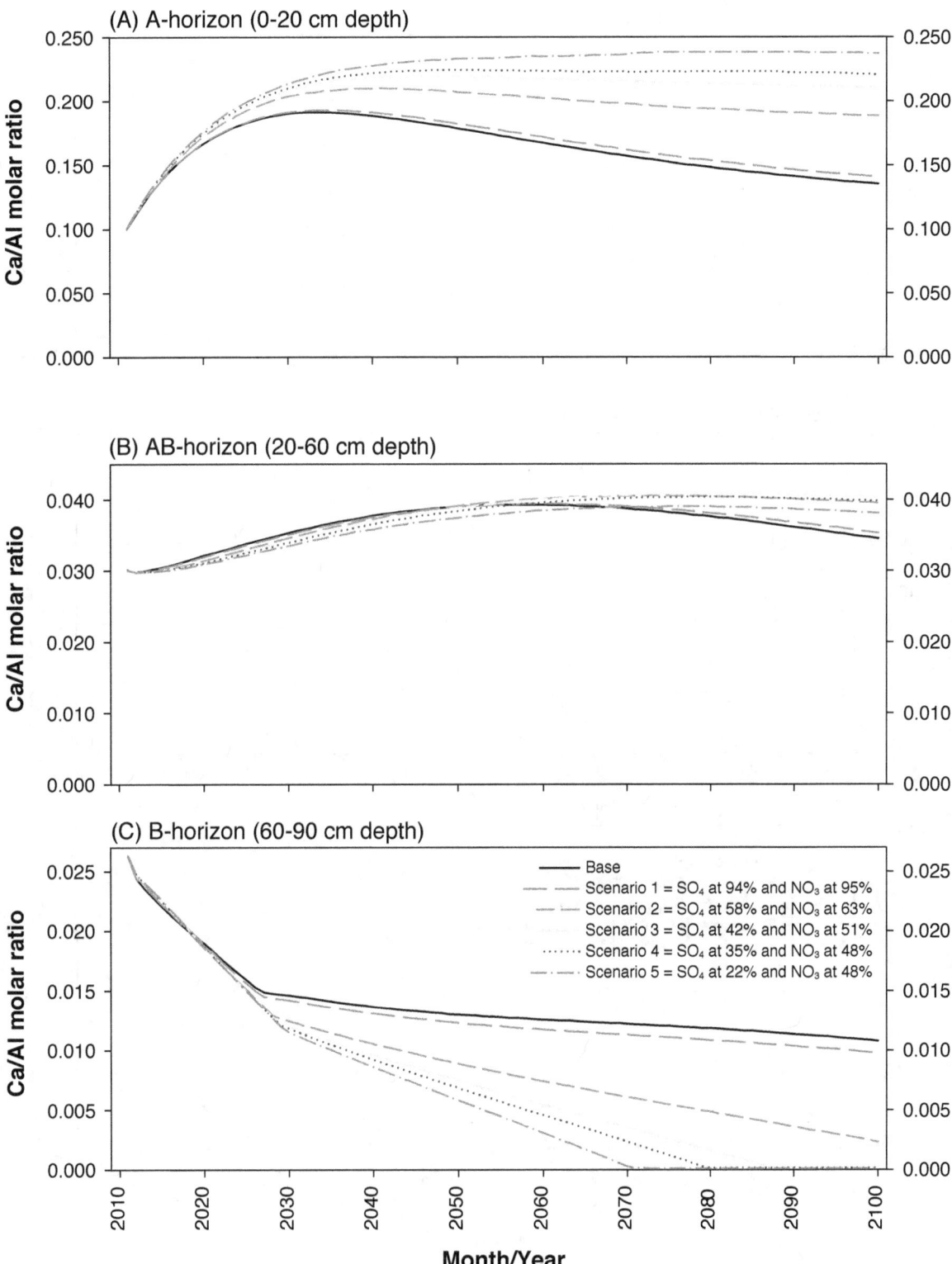

Figure 10—Simulated soil Ca/Al molar ratio for the five deposition scenarios compared to the current deposition (base) for Shining Rock Wilderness. The five scenarios were based on percentages of the current condition.

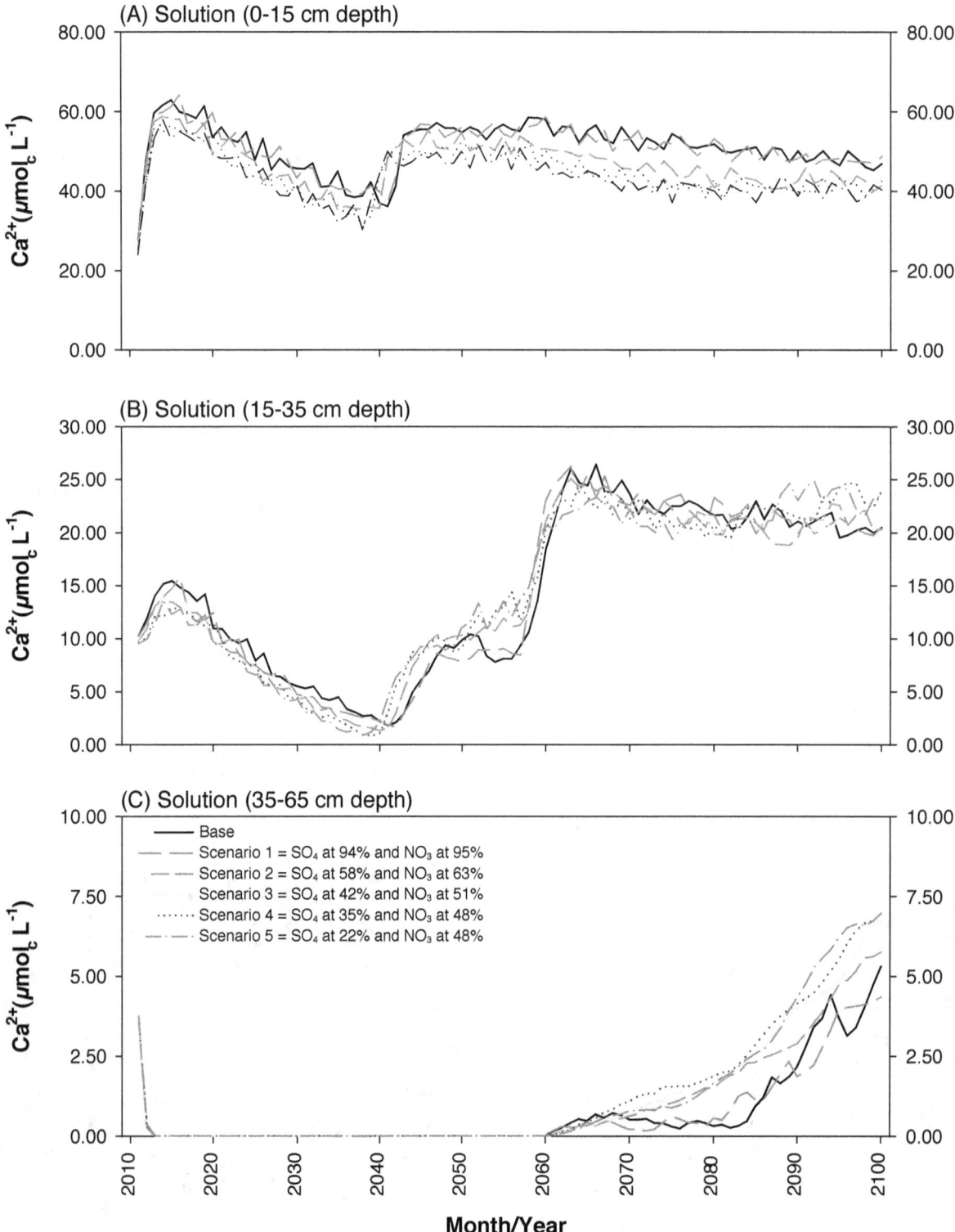

Figure 11—Simulated soil solution calcium (Ca²⁺) for the five deposition scenarios compared to the current deposition (base) for Linville Gorge Wilderness. The five scenarios were based on percentages of the current condition.

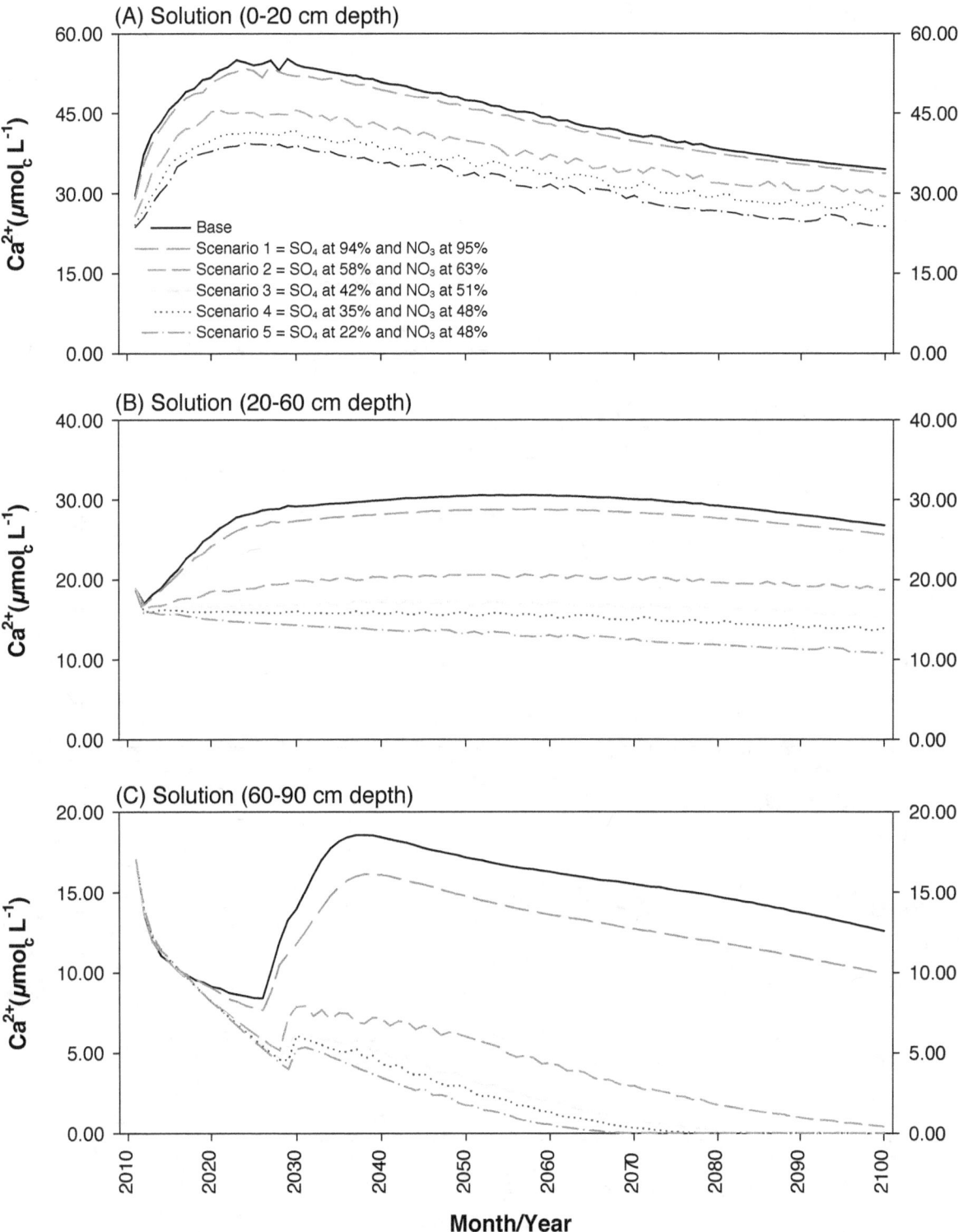

Figure 12—Simulated soil solution calcium (Ca²⁺) for the five deposition scenarios compared to the current deposition (base) for Shining Rock Wilderness. The five scenarios were based on percentages of the current condition.

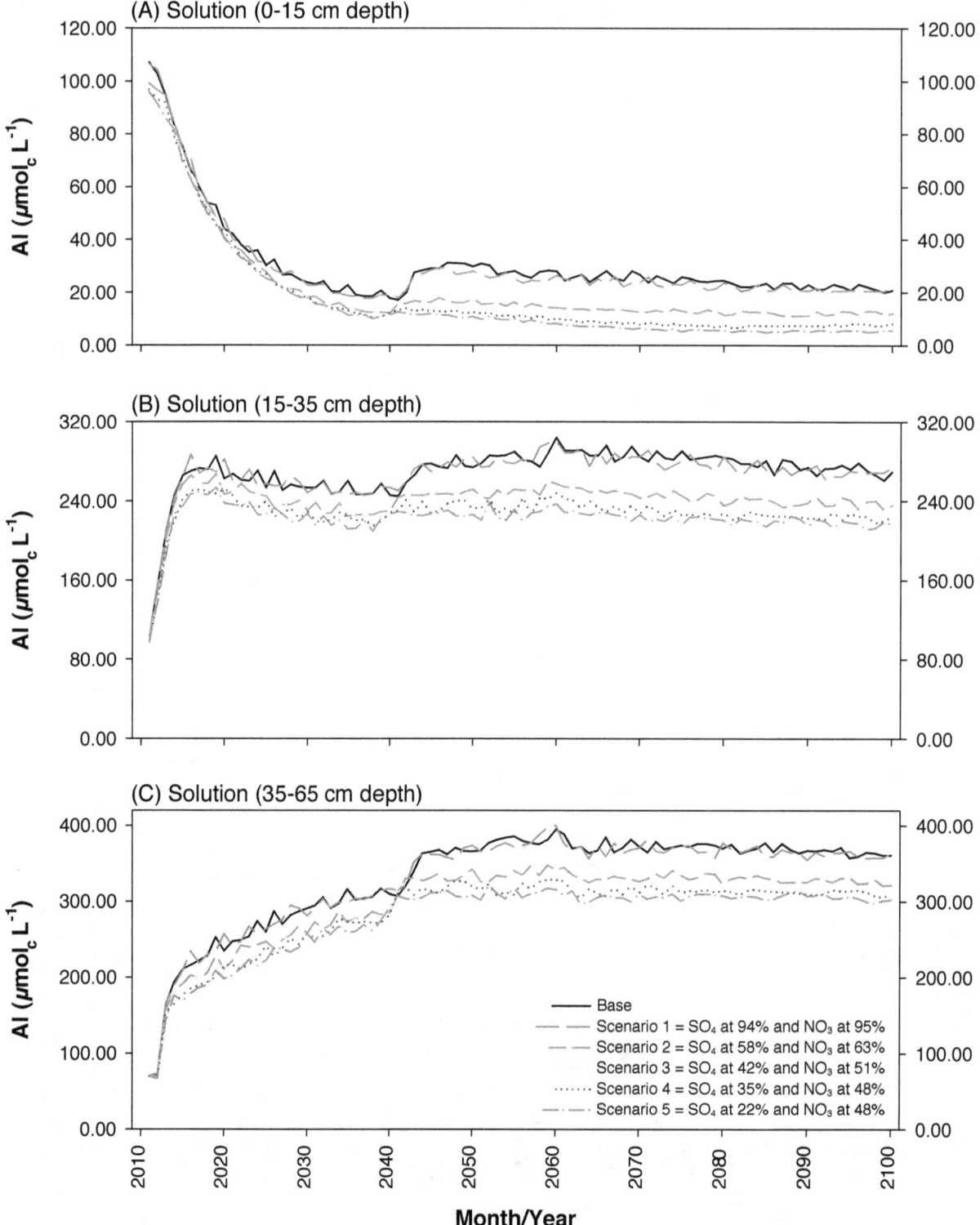

Figure 13—Simulated soil solution aluminum (Al) for the five deposition scenarios compared to the current deposition (base) for Linville Gorge Wilderness. The five scenarios were based on percentages of the current condition.

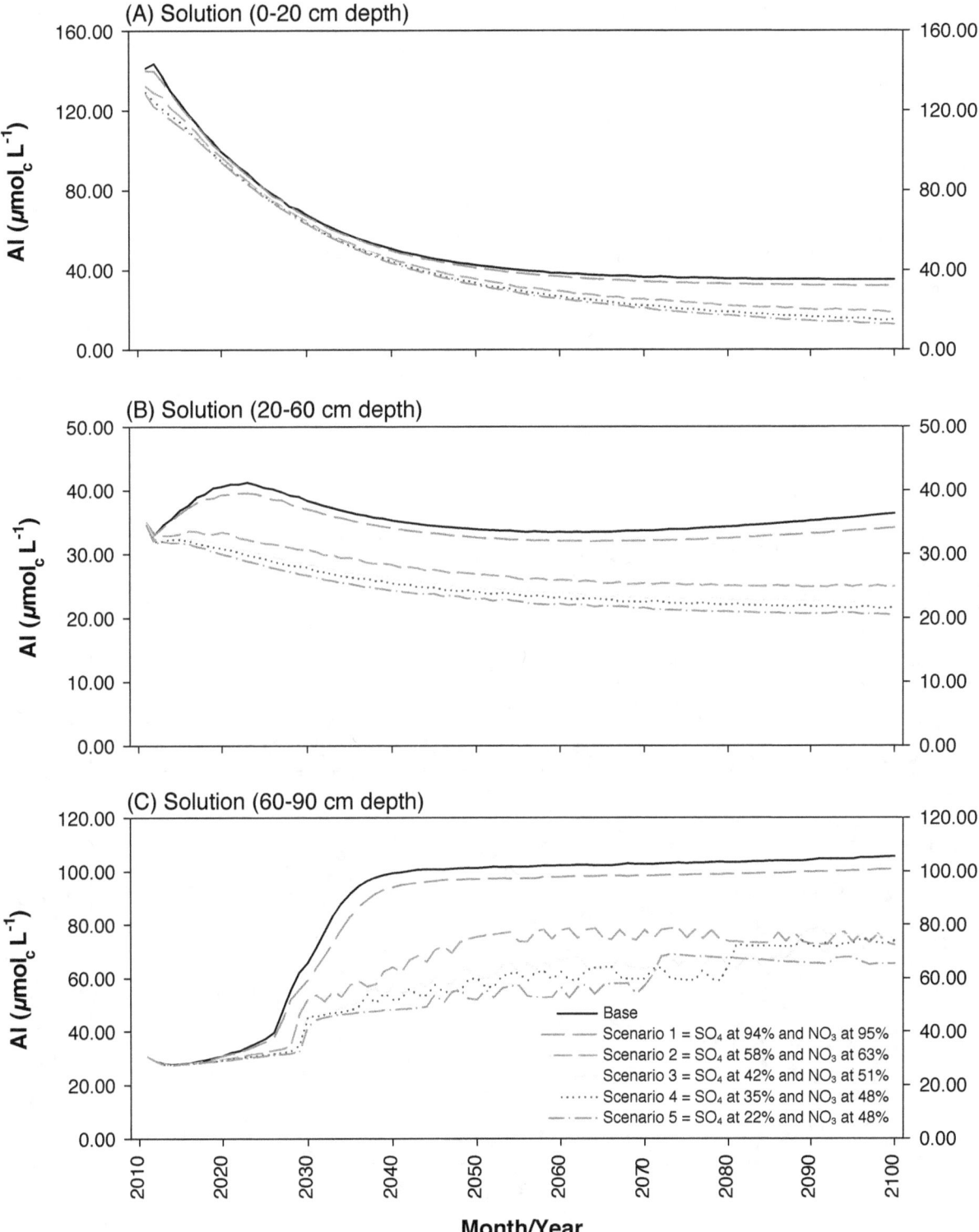

Figure 14—Simulated soil solution aluminum (Al) for the five deposition scenarios compared to the current deposition (base) for Shining Rock Wilderness. The five scenarios were based on percentages of the current condition.

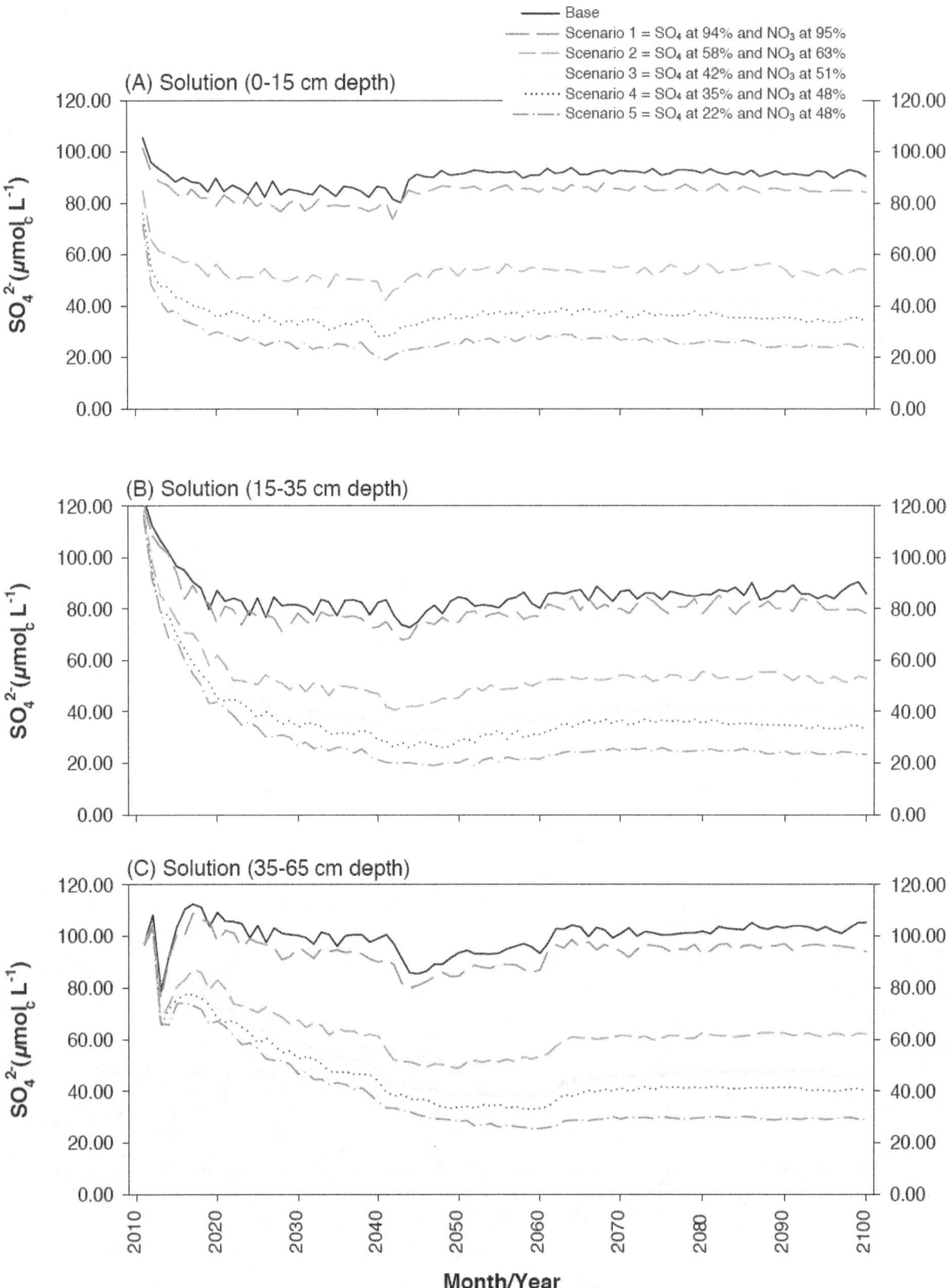

Figure 15—Simulated soil solution sulfate (SO₄²⁻) for the five deposition scenarios compared to the current deposition (base) for Linville Gorge Wilderness. The five scenarios were based on percentages of the current condition.

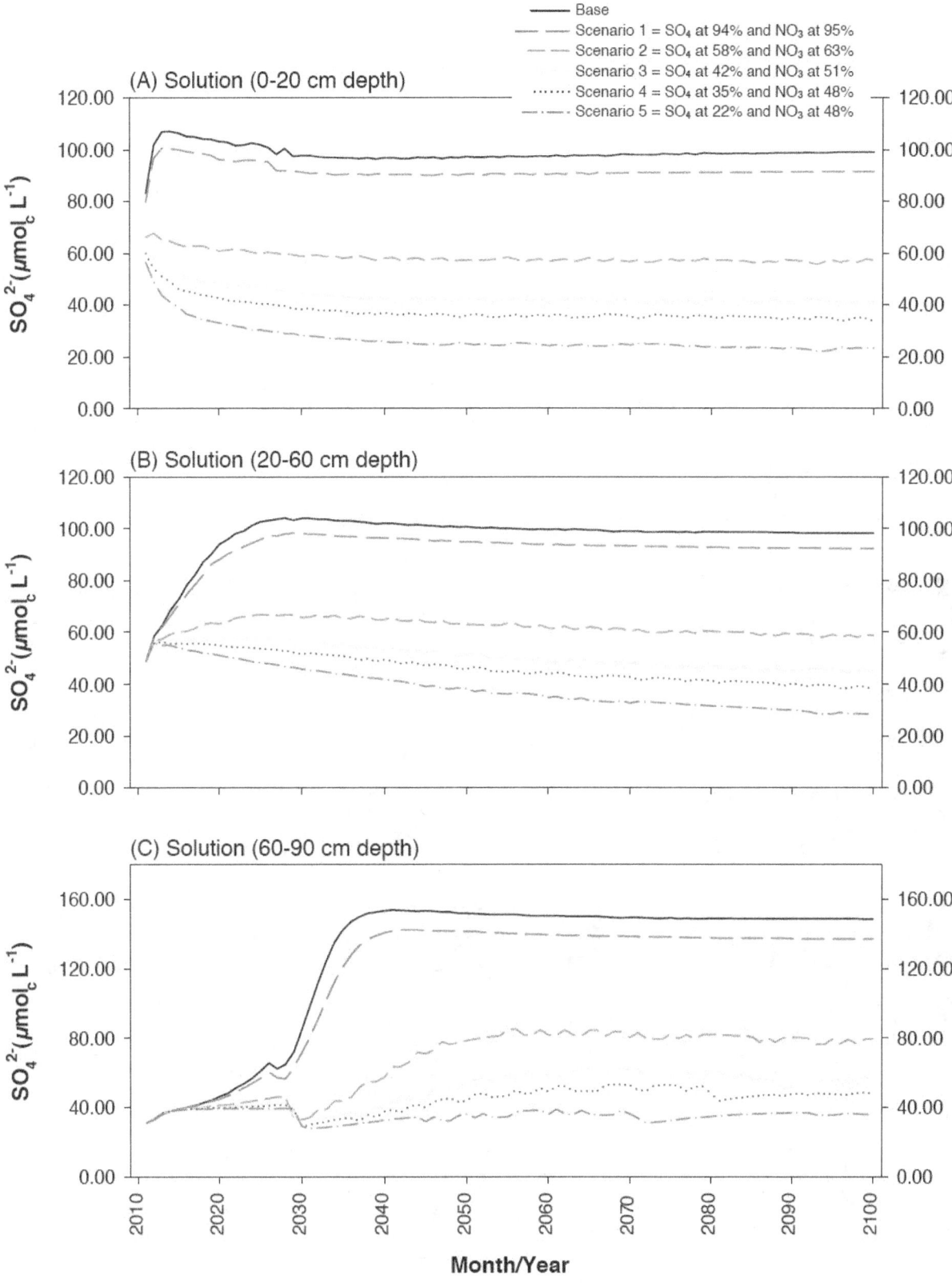

Figure 16—Simulated soil solution sulfate (SO_4^{2-}) for the five deposition scenarios compared to the current deposition (base) for Shining Rock Wilderness. The five scenarios were based on percentages of the current condition.

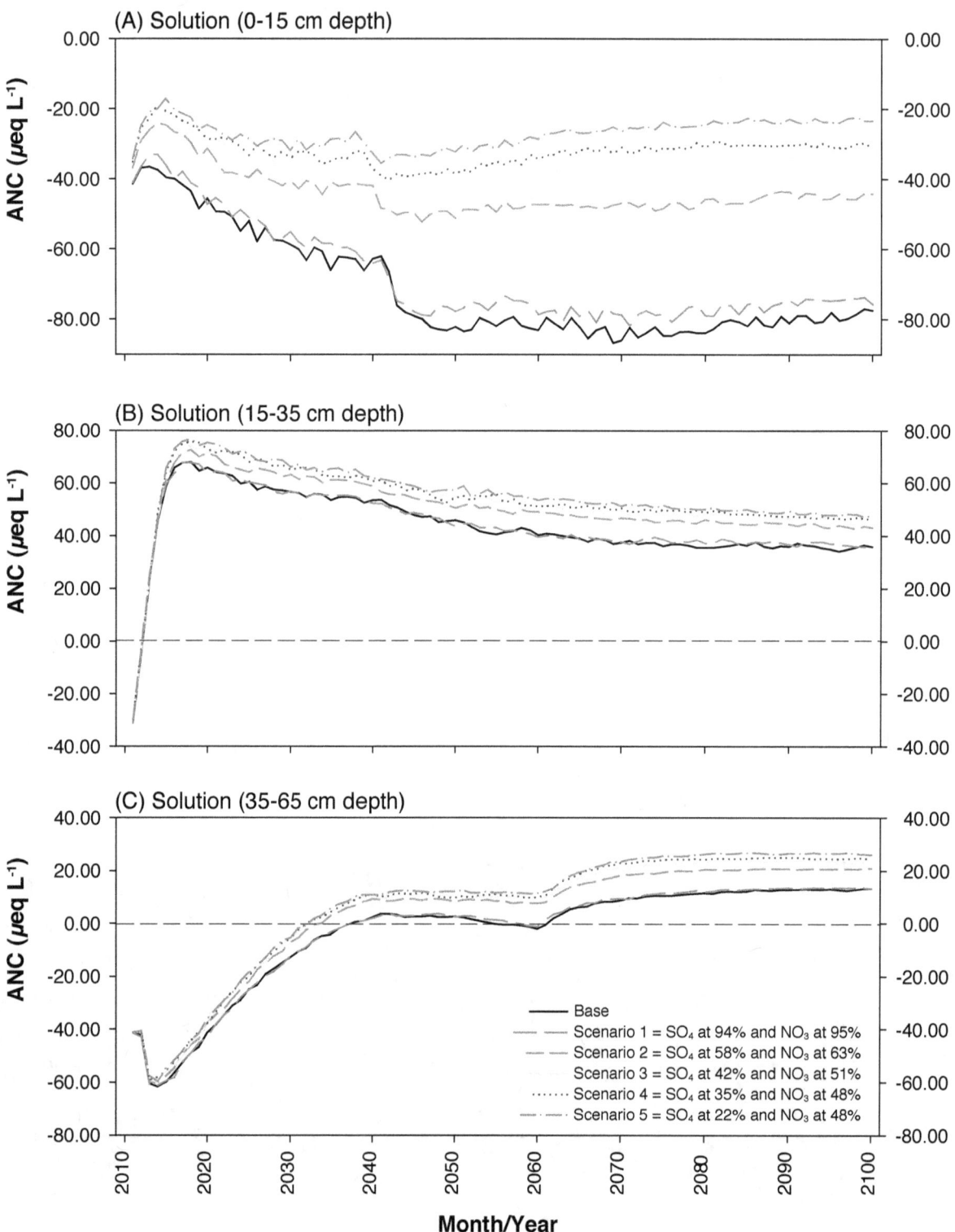

Figure 17—Simulated soil solution anion neutralizing capacity (ANC) for the five deposition scenarios compared to the current deposition (base) for Linville Gorge Wilderness. The five scenarios were based on percentages of the current condition.

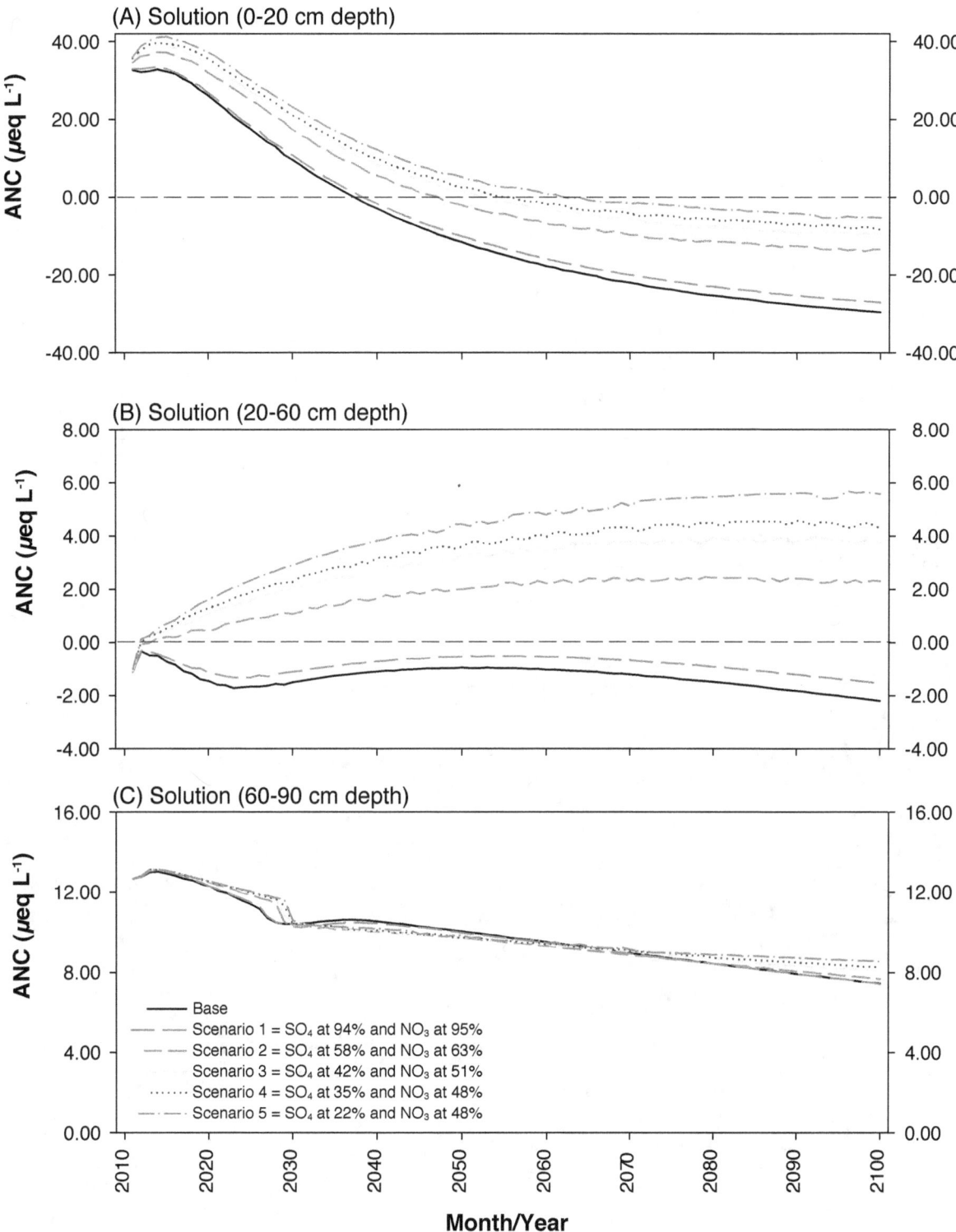

Figure 18—Simulated soil solution anion neutralizing capacity (ANC) for the five deposition scenarios compared to the current deposition (base) for Shining Rock Wilderness. The five scenarios were based on percentages of the current condition.

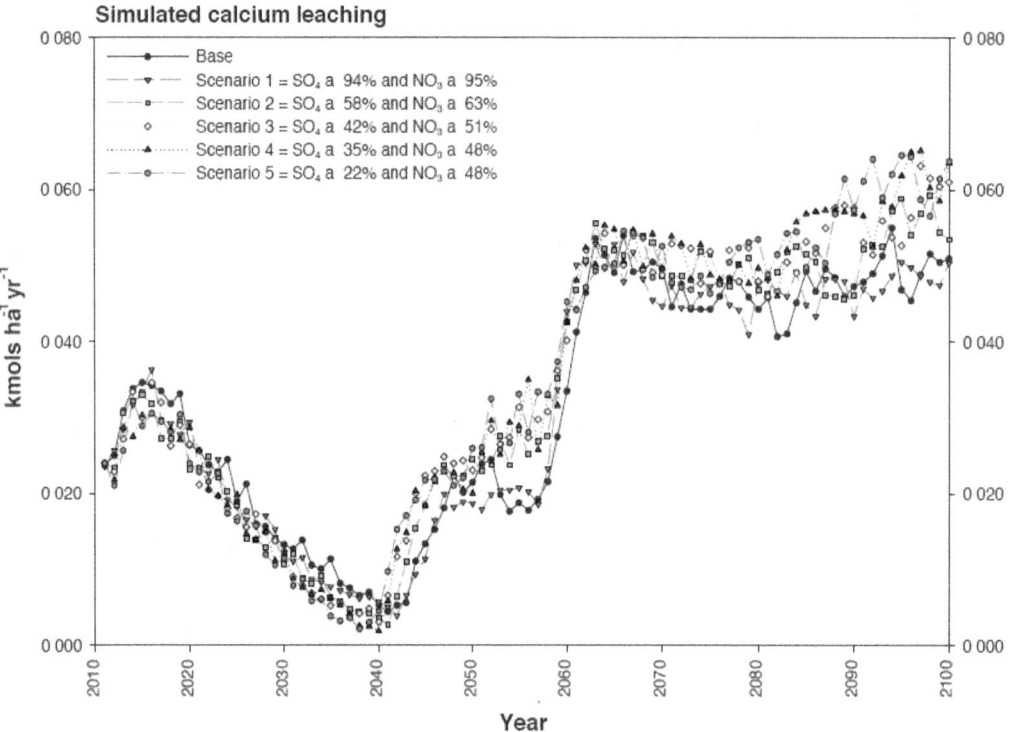

Figure 19—Simulated calcium (Ca²⁺) leaching for the five deposition scenarios compared to the current deposition (base) for Linville Gorge Wilderness. The five scenarios were based on percentages of the current condition.

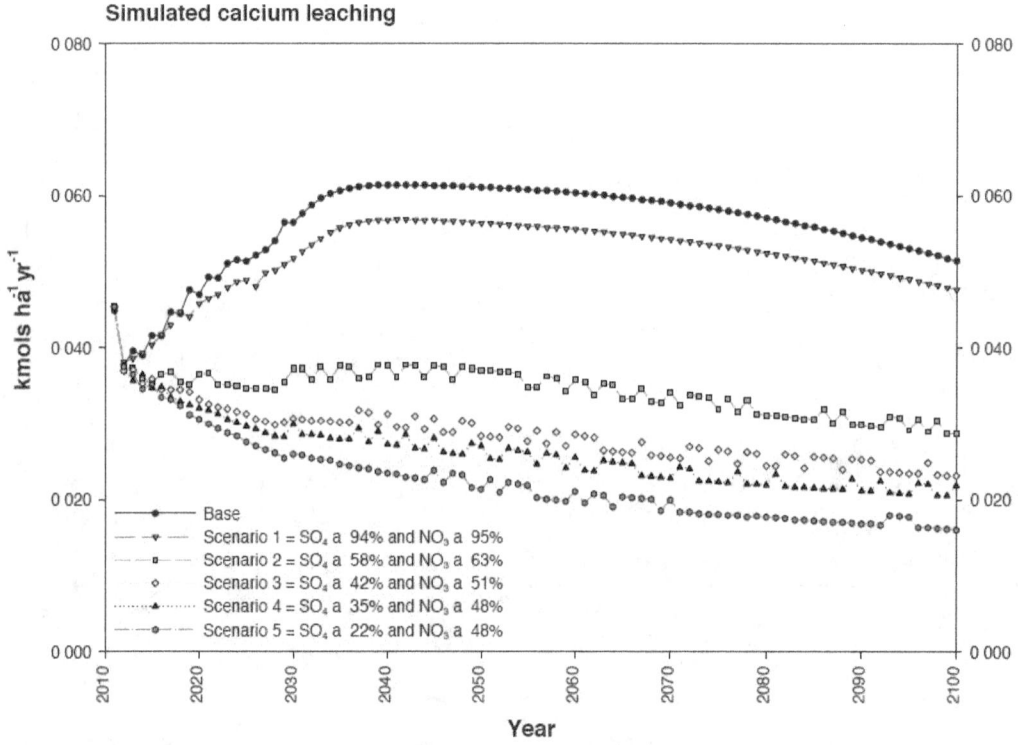

Figure 20—Simulated calcium (Ca²⁺) leaching for the five deposition scenarios compared to the current deposition (base) for Shining Rock Wilderness. The five scenarios were based on percentages of the current condition.

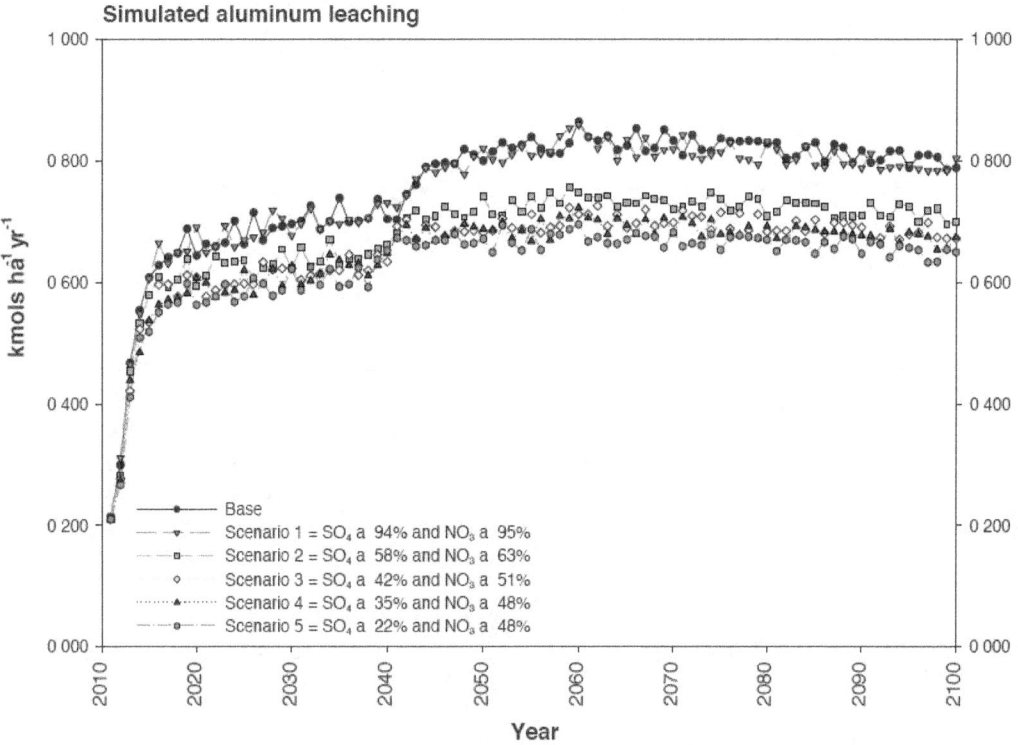

Figure 21—Simulated aluminum (Al) leaching for the five deposition scenarios compared to the current deposition (base) for Linville Gorge Wilderness. The five scenarios were based on percentages of the current condition.

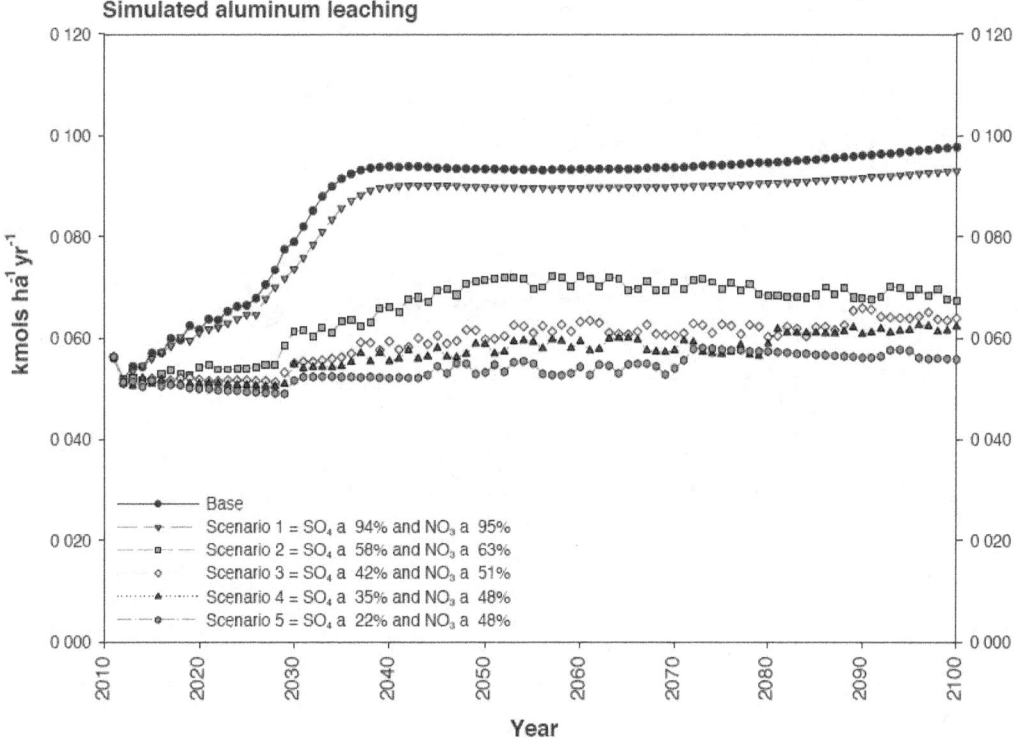

Figure 22—Simulated aluminum (Al) leaching for the five deposition scenarios compared to the current deposition (base) for Shining Rock Wilderness. The five scenarios were based on percentages of the current condition.

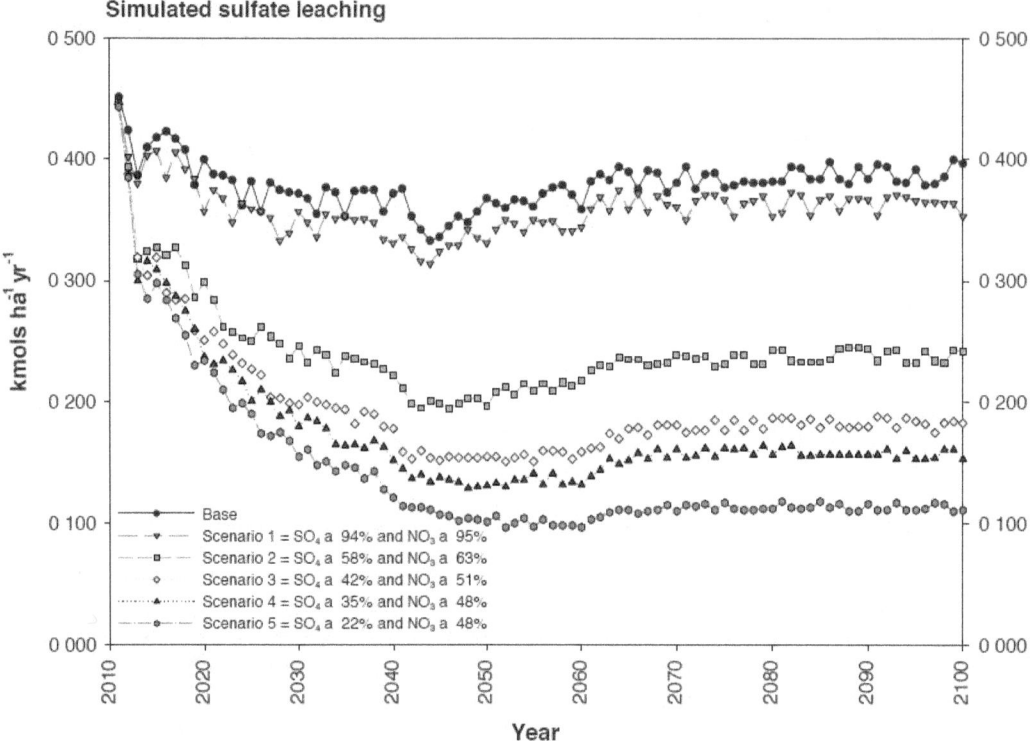

Figure 23—Simulated sulfate (SO_4^{2-}) leaching for the five deposition scenarios compared to current deposition (base) for Linville Gorge Wilderness. The five scenarios were based on percentages of the current condition.

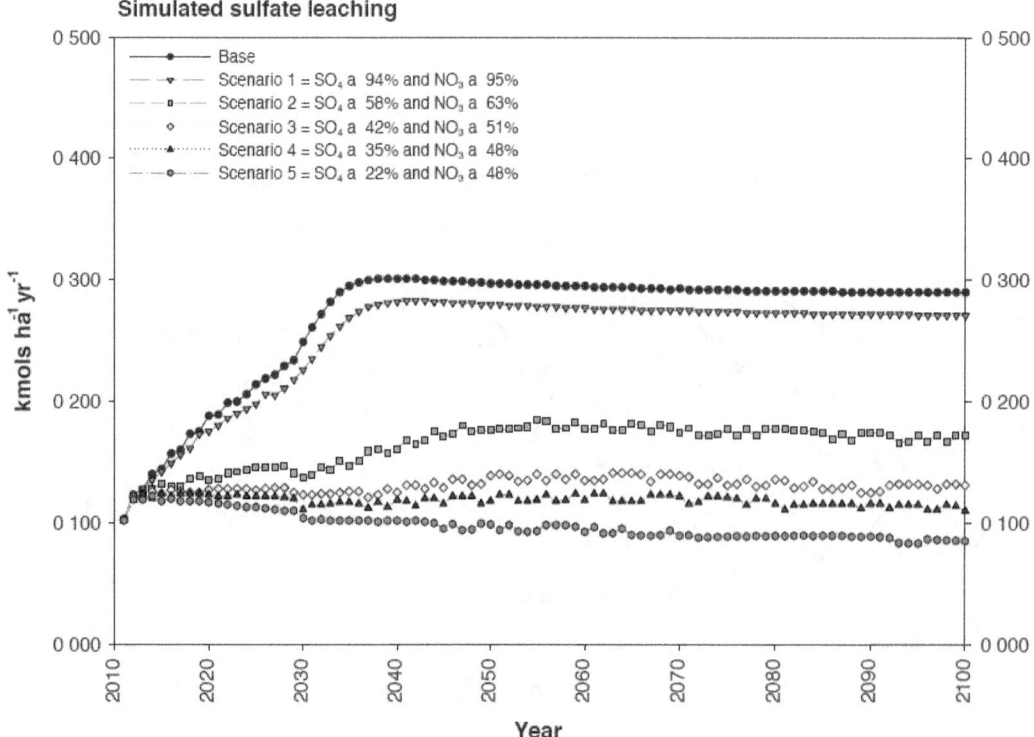

Figure 24—Simulated sulfate (SO_4^{2-}) leaching for the five deposition scenarios compared to the current deposition (base) for Shining Rock Wilderness. The five scenarios were based on percentages of the current condition.

SUMMARY

Anthropogenic emissions of sulfur dioxide (SO_2) in North America have shown marked temporal changes over the past 100 years with a maximum occurring in the early 1970s followed by a substantial decline (Mitchell and others 2011). Much of this decline in the U.S. was driven by the enactment of the Clean Air Act in 1970 and subsequent Title IV Amendment of the Clean Air Act in 1990 (Scenario 1), as well as other regulatory controls on SO_2 emissions (CAIR, Scenario 2 and implementation of the Regional Haze Rule). Elevated S deposition has been closely linked with the acidification of soils and surface waters (Elliott and others 2008). This acidification has resulted in the mobilization of toxic cations (e.g., aluminum) (Driscoll and Postek 1996) and the depletion of soil nutrient cations (e.g., Ca^{2+}, Mg^{2+}) (Bailey and others 2005, Elliott and others 2008).

Large reductions in SO_2 are anticipated between 2002 and 2018 along with substantial NO_x reductions from utilities. If the deposition reductions equate to SO_4^{2-} of at least 78 percent and NO_3^- of 52 percent (Scenario 5) then improvements in future percent BS is anticipated at both wildernesses. In the rooting zone, the soil exchangeable Ca^{2+} will continue to remain low and the amount of Al in soil solution is predicted to decrease, but will still be very high at LGW. The high concentrations of Al are of concern because the amount could be toxic to fine roots. Mortality of the fine roots decreases the surface area for water absorption and may lead to decreases in the amount of base cation uptake (especially Ca^{2+}) required to support healthy vegetation. Forecasted reductions in acidic deposition for LGW and SRW are also likely to improve conditions for aquatic biota as evidenced by a decrease in the amount of Al leaching from the soils and an increase in the soil solution ANC.

There are two pieces of information that would aid future studies to determine the level of acidic deposition that can be tolerated by Appalachian ecosystems. First, the State air quality agencies in the Southeastern United States are conducting joint atmospheric dispersion modeling of current and future emissions. It would be very useful to obtain the total SO_4^{2-} and NO_3^- deposition estimates to use in future analysis with NuCM or a similar type of biogeochemical model. Second, land managers need to continue receiving instruction on acidic deposition impacts so they can advise air regulatory agencies on what level of total SO_4^{2-} and NO_3^- deposition the ecosystem can tolerate for long-term sustainability. The two wildernesses in this study do represent some of the other high elevation areas in the Southern Appalachians. Land managers need to understand there is a possibility that other areas, such as these two wildernesses, may not fully recover within a desired time period, even with additional reductions in acidic deposition. The extent of these areas is not known at this time; however, the identified acidic forests should be considered for restoration with nutrient supplements (such as liming) to replace deficient base cations (especially Ca^{2+}) in order to move towards a healthier ecosystem.

ACKNOWLEDGMENTS

We thank the Pisgah and Grandfather Ranger Districts, Pisgah National Forest for their cooperation in establishing field sites. Special thanks to Patsy Clinton, Chris Sobek, Neal Muldoon, and Jason Love for assistance in field sampling and Cindi Brown and Carol Harper for chemical analyses of samples. Drs. Todd McDonnell and Wei Wu provided helpful comments on the manuscript. This research was supported by Region 8, USDA Forest Service; Coweeta Hydrologic Laboratory, Southern Research Station, USDA Forest Service; and the Coweeta LTER project funded by National Science Foundation grant DEB-0823293.

LITERATURE CITED

Bailey, S.W.; Horsley, S.B.; Long, R.P. 2005. Thirty years of change in forest soils of the Allegheny Plateau, Pennsylvania. Soil Science Society of America Journal. 69:681-690.

Baker, L.A.; Kauffman, P.R.; Herlihy, A.T.; Eilers, J.M. 1990. Acidic deposition: current status of surface water acid-base chemistry. NAPAP Rep. 9. Washington, DC: National Acid Precipitation Assessment Program. Vol. II. 367 pp.

Bulger, A.J ; Cosby, B.J.; Doloff, C.A. [and others]. 1999. Shenandoah National Park: fish in sensitive habitats. Final report. An integrated assessment of fish community responses to stream acidification. Charlottesville, VA: University of Virgina. Cooperative Agreement CA-4000-2-1007, Supplemental Agreement #2.

Byun, D.W ; Ching, J.K.S. 1999. Science algorithms of the EPA Models-3 Community Multiscale Air Quality (CMAQ) modeling system. EPA/600/R-99/030. Washington, DC: Environmental Protection Agency, Office of Research and Development. 767 pp.

Clescerl, L.S.; Greenberg, A.E.; Eaton, A.D. 1999. Standard methods for the examination of water and wastewater, 20th edition. Washington, DC: American Public Health Assoc./American Water Works Assoc./Water Environment Federation. 1325 pp.

Cosby, B.J.; Webb, J.R.; Galloway, J.N.; Deviney, F.A. 2006. Acidic deposition impacts on natural resources in Shenandoah National Park. Technical Report NPS/NER/NRTR-2006/066. Philadelphia, PA: U.S. Department of the Interior, National Park Service, Northeast Region. 167 pp. + apps.

Driscoll, C.T.; Postek, K.M. 1996. The chemistry of aluminum in surface waters. In: Sposito, G., ed. The environmental chemistry of aluminum. Boca Raton, FL: CRC Press: 363-418.

Driscoll, C.T.; Lawrence, G.B.; Bulger, A.J. [and others]. 2001. Acidic deposition in the northeastern United States: sources and inputs, ecosystem effects, and management strategies. BioScience. 51:180-198.

Driscoll, C.T.; Driscoll, K.M.; Mitchell, M.J.; Raynal, D.J. 2003. Effects of acidic deposition on forest and aquatic ecosystems in New York State. Environmental Pollution. 123:327-336.

Elliott, K.J.; Vose, J.M.; Knoepp, J.D. [and others]. 2008. Simulated effects of sulfur deposition on nutrient cycling in class I wilderness areas. Journal of Environmental Quality. 37:1419-1431.

Farr, C.; Skousen, J.; Edwards, P. [and others]. 2009. Acid soil indicators in forest soils of the Cherry River Watershed, West Virginia. Environmental Monitoring and Assessment. 158:343-353.

Halman, J.M; Schaberg, P.G.; Hawley, G.J.; Hansen, C.F. 2011. Potential role of soil calcium in recovery of paper birch following ice storm injury in Vermont, USA. Forest Ecology and Management. 261:1539-1545.

Johnson, D.W.; Lindberg, S.E., eds. 1992. Atmospheric deposition and forest nutrient cycling: a synthesis of the integrated forest study. Ecological Series 91. New York: Springer-Verlag. 707 pp.

Johnson, D.W.; Susfalk, R.B.; Brewer, P.F.; Swank, W.T. 1999. Simulated effects of reduced sulfur, nitrogen, and base cation deposition on soils and solutions in Southern Appalachian forests. Journal of Environmental Quality. 28:1336-1346.

Johnson, D.W.; Todd, D.E ; Trettin, C.F.; Mulholland, P.J. 2008. Decadal changes in potassium, calcium, and magnesium in a deciduous forest soil. Soil Science Society of America Journal. 72:1795-1805.

Liu, S.A.; Munsen, R.K.; Johnson, D.W. [and others]. 1991a. The Nutrient Cycling Model (NuCM): overview and application. In: Johnson, D.S.; Lindberg, S.E., eds. Atmospheric deposition and forest nutrient cycling: a synthesis of the integrated forest study. Ecological Studies 91. New York: Springer-Verlag. 583-609.

Liu, S.A.; Munsen, R.K.; Johnson, D.W. [and others]. 1991b. Applications of a nutrient cycling model (NuCM) to a northern mixed hardwood and a southern coniferous forest. Tree Physiology. 9:173-182.

Long, R.P.; Horsley, S.B.; Hall, T.J. 2011. Long-term impact of liming on growth and vigor of northern hardwoods. Canadian Journal of Forest Research. 41:1295-1307.

Markewitz, D.; Richter, D.D.; Allen, H.L.; Urrego, J.B. 1998. Three decades of observed soil acidification in the Calhoun Experimental Forest: has acid rain made a difference? Soil Science Society of America Journal 62:1428-1439.

Mitchell, M.J.; Lovett, G.; Bailey, S. [and others]. 2011. Comparisons of watershed sulfur budgets in southeast Canada and northeast US: new approaches and implications. Biogeochemistry 103:181-207.

Munsen, R.K.; Liu, S.; Gherini, S.A. [and others]. 1992. NuCM code version 2.0: an IBM PC code for simulating nutrient cycling in forest ecosystems. Hadley, MA: Tetra-Tech.

National Atmospheric Deposition Program (NADP). 1998. National Atmospheric Deposition Program 1997 Wet Deposition. Champaign, IL: Illinois State Water Survey. 16 pp.

National Acid Precipitation Assessment Program (NAPAP). 2005. National Acid Precipitation Assessment Program report to Congress: an integrated assessment. Washington, DC: National Science and Technology Council. 85 pp. Available at www.napap.noaa.gov/reports.

Newell, C.L.; Peet, R.K. 1995. Vegetation of Linville Gorge Wilderness, North Carolina. Curriculum in Ecology & Department of Biology. Chapel Hill, NC: University of North Carolina at Chapel Hill. 211 pp.

Newell, C.L.; Peet, R.K. 1996. Vegetation of Shining Rock Wilderness, North Carolina. Curriculum in Ecology & Department of Biology. Chapel Hill, NC: University of North Carolina at Chapel Hill. 253 pp.

NOAA. 1999. National Climatic Data Center: daily surface data (primarily U.S.). Documentation Manual, U.S. Department of Commerce. Washington, DC: National Oceanic and Atmospheric Administration.

Robinson, R.B.; Wood, M.S.; Smoot, J.L.; Moore, S.E. 2003. Parametric modeling of water quality and sampling strategy in a high-altitude Appalachian stream. Journal of Hydrology. 14:24-37.

Schaberg, P.G.; Tilley, J.W.; Hawley, G.J. [and others]. 2006. Associations of calcium and aluminum with the growth and health of sugar maple trees in Vermont. Forest Ecology and Management. 223:159-169.

Sullivan, T.J.; Cosby, B.J.; Herlihy, A.T. [and others]. 2004. Regional model projections of future effects of sulfur and nitrogen deposition on streams in the Southern Appalachian Mountains. Water Resources Research. 40: W02101 doi:02110.01029/02003WR001998.

Sullivan, T.J.; Cosby, B.J.; Jackson, W.A. 2011a. Target loads of atmospheric sulfur deposition for the protection and recovery of acid-sensitive streams in the Southern Blue Ridge Province. Journal of Environmental Management. 11: 2953-2960. doi:10.1016/j.jenvman.2011.07.014.

Sullivan, T.J.; Cosby, B. J.; Jackson, W.A. [and others]. 2011b. Acidification and prognosis for future recovery of acid-sensitive streams in the Southern Blue Ridge Province. Water, Air, & Soil Pollution. 219:11-26.

Swank, W.T.; Waide, J.B. 1988. Characterization of baseline precipitation and stream chemistry and nutrient budgets for control watersheds. In: Swank, W.T.; Crossley, D.A. Jr., eds. Forest Hydrology and Ecology at Coweeta. Ecological Studies 66. New York: Springer-Verlag. 57-79.

Vanderzanden, D.; Lachowski, H.; Jackson, B ; Clerke, B. 1999. Mapping vegetation in the Southern Appalachians with multidate satellite imagery: a wilderness case study. U.S. Department of Agriculture Forest Service, Engineering, Remote Sensing Application Center. RSAC-2300-IRS-0009-RPT1. 33 pp.

Vose, J.M.; Swank, W.T. 1991. A soil temperature model for closed canopied forest stands. Research Paper SE-281. Asheville, NC: U.S. Department of Agriculture Forest Service, Southeastern Forest Experiment Station. 11 pp.

Elliott, K.J.; Vose, J.M.; Jackson, W.A. 2013. Effects of future sulfate and nitrate deposition scenarios on Linville Gorge and Shining Rock Wildernesses. Gen. Tech. Rep. SRS-181. Asheville, NC: U.S. Department of Agriculture Forest Service, Southern Research Station. 30 p.

We used the Nutrient Cycling Model (NuCM) to simulate the effects of various sulfur (S) and nitrogen (N) deposition scenarios on wilderness areas in Western North Carolina. Linville Gorge Wilderness (LGW) and Shining Rock Wilderness (SRW) were chosen because they are high elevation acidic cove forests and are located on geologic parent material known to be low in base cations and thus sensitive to acidic deposition. We used five sulfate (SO_4^{2-}) and nitrate (NO_3^-) deposition scenarios to compare with the current (base case) deposition: Scenario 1, SO_4^{2-} at 94 percent and NO_3^- at 95 percent of current deposition; Scenario 2, SO_4^{2-} at 58 percent and NO_3^- at 63 percent; Scenario 3, SO_4^{2-} at 42 percent and NO_3^- at 51 percent; Scenario 4, SO_4^{2-} at 35 percent and NO_3^- at 48 percent; and Scenario 5, SO_4^{2-} at 22 percent and NO_3^- at 48 percent. For both sites, soil exchangeable calcium (Ca^{2+}) increased while exchangeable aluminum (Al^{3+}) changed very little over the 90-year simulation period with greater reductions in SO_4^{2-} and NO_3^- deposition; and the increase in soil exchangeable Ca^{2+} improved soil Ca/Al molar ratios. Soil solution SO_4^{2-} was much lower at all soil depths with greater reductions in SO_4^{2-} and NO_3^- deposition. This reduction in SO_4^{2-} in solution resulted in greater soil solution acid neutralizing capacity (ANC). At LGW, soil solution ANC of shallow soil was improved with the deposition Scenarios 2-5 compared to current deposition. By 2040, solution ANC of deep soil had increased above 20 μeq L^{-1} for Scenarios 3-5 at LGW suggesting that stream ANC will be improved as well with further reductions in acidic deposition. Soil and solution cation concentrations will be improved for both wildernesses based on Scenario 2; however, further reductions in acidic deposition (e.g., Scenario 5) will be needed to increase stream ANC to a level that could support trout and other fishes.

Keywords: Atmospheric deposition, calcium, forecasting, nitrogen, Nutrient Cycling Model, Southern Appalachians.

How do you rate this publication?

Scan this code to submit your feedback or go to www.srs.fs.usda.gov/pubeval

Non-Discrimination Policy
The U.S. Department of Agriculture (USDA) prohibits discrimination against its customers, employees, and applicants for employment on the bases of race, color, national origin, age, disability, sex, gender identity, religion, reprisal, and where applicable, political beliefs, marital status, familial or parental status, sexual orientation, or all or part of an individual's income is derived from any public assistance program, or protected genetic information in employment or in any program or activity conducted or funded by the Department. (Not all prohibited bases will apply to all programs and/or employment activities.)

To File an Employment Complaint
If you wish to file an employment complaint, you must contact your agency's EEO Counselor within 45 days of the date of the alleged discriminatory act, event, or in the case of a personnel action. Additional information can be found online at http://www.ascr.usda.gov/complaint_filing_file html.

To File a Program Complaint
If you wish to file a Civil Rights program complaint of discrimination, complete the USDA Program Discrimination Complaint Form, found online at http://www.ascr.usda.gov/complaint_filing_cust html, or at any USDA office, or call (866) 632-9992 to request the form. You may also write a letter containing all of the information requested in the form. Send your completed complaint form or letter to us by mail at U.S. Department of Agriculture, Director, Office of Adjudication, 1400 Independence Avenue, S.W., Washington, D.C. 20250-99410, by fax (202) 690-7442 or email at program.intake@usda.gov.

Persons with Disabilities
Individuals who are deaf, hard of hearing or have speech disabilities and you wish to file either an EEO or program complaint please contact USDA through the Federal Relay Service at (800) 877-8339 or (800) 845-6136 (in Spanish).

Persons with disabilities who wish to file a program complaint, please see information above on how to contact us by mail directly or by email. If you require alternative means of communication for program information (e.g., Braille, large print, audiotape, etc.) please contact USDA's TARGET Center at (202) 720-2600 (voice and TDD).

www.ingramcontent.com/pod-product-compliance
Lightning Source LLC
Chambersburg PA
CBHW080640290526
45790CB00007B/3151